PRESENTED TO:

Faye Fraynelis

BY:

Lynne Owen

DATE:

Sept 28, 2018

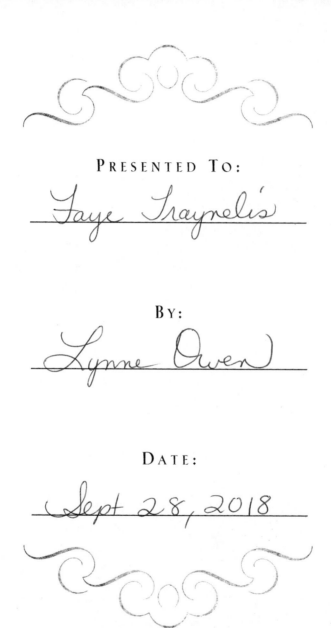

Seasons of Love

Celebrating the Tender Moments of Life

Karen Hardin

WHITE STONE BOOKS
LAKELAND, FLORIDA

Unless otherwise noted as an excerpt from previously published articles, all interviews were conducted by and manuscript written by Karen Hardin in conjunction with White Stone Books, Inc.

07 06 05 10 9 8 7 6 5 4 3 2 1

Seasons of Love:
Celebrating the Tender Moments of Life
ISBN 1-59379-022-8

P. O. Box 700515
Tulsa, Oklahoma 74170-0515

Published by White Stone Books, Inc.
P.O. Box 2835
Lakeland, Florida 33806

Project editor: Betsy Williams, williams.services.inc@cox.net

Dedication

To my three treasures—Michael, Holly, and Joshua. Because of you I've experienced a depth of love that I didn't know existed.

And to Kevin, the love of my life.

Special Note of Appreciation

To Venicia and Michelle—your encouragement and willingness to help have been greatly appreciated. I love you.

To Debbie Justus Collins and the White Stone Books team—for your investments and amazing dedication.

CONTENTS

Now these three remain: faith, hope and love.
But the greatest of these is love.

1 CORINTHIANS 13:13

Seasons of Love

Celebrating the Tender Moments of Life

INTRODUCTION

Three-year-old Joshua was running across the room after his older sister, Holly, when he abruptly changed course and ran to where I was sitting at the computer. Throwing his little arms around me, he exclaimed, "I wuv you, Mommy!" After a quick squeeze, he scampered back to Holly, jumping right back into play. I, however, couldn't jump right back into my work.

Wow! It took just five seconds of his time to make my day. It was such a tender, yet unexpected moment. Unlike our nightly prayers followed by hugs and kisses or an expression of love because we had given him a toy, this was just a simple display from the heart of our little guy who stopped everything he was doing...just because. It is moments like this that I have tried to capture in the stories of *Seasons of Love.*

Love comes in many shapes and sizes. It is indiscriminate of age, gender, or race, sprinkling our lives with tender emotion even in the hardest individuals—sometimes showing up where you least expect it. But even when the embrace lasts only a moment—as it did with my son—love leaves an indelible mark.

The English language uses and abuses the word "love." Yet if you refer to the same word in the Greek language—the language in which the New Testament was originally written—you find a more finely tuned breakdown of the word, conveying love at four different levels. *Eros, storgos, phileo,* and *agapé* can all be translated "love" in English; but each represents a distinctly different facet of love.

The first, *eros,* is where we get the word "erotic." Unfortunately, it is this lowest form of love that our society has such a voracious appetite for and consumes in large doses. *Eros* is indeed pleasurable, but it is a self-seeking, self-gratifying love. Incapable of providing lasting fulfillment, it is not the true love for which our hearts ultimately yearn.

Storgos, simply stated, is a form of devotion. It is the type of love we have for our pets, that is shared between siblings, or that a parent has for a child. Platonic in nature, yet its river runs deep, creating a bond between individuals that is not easily broken.

Phileo is the affectionate love shared among friends or between a boyfriend and girlfriend. It is the foundation of a well-suited match, a love that can grow much deeper as a relationship develops. It is the same word from which we derive the name "Philadelphia," the City of Brotherly Love.

Finally, the highest form of love is *agapé*. It is a perfect, sacrificial love—superhuman. It is a love that our selfish, human nature can never match, but was exemplified when our Creator gave His only begotten Son. It is this love that He sheds abroad in our hearts when we make Jesus our Lord.

Although God often uses people to express it, all love emanates from Him. And because He wants us to experience it in all its fullness, He lavishly showers it upon us through all *the seasons of love.*

Dear friends, let us love one another, for love comes from God.

1 JOHN 4:7–8

Friendship

A friend is someone who knows the song
in your heart and can sing it back to you
when you have forgotten the words.

AUTHOR UNKNOWN

SECTION 1

Puppy Love

With most folks the dog stands highest
as man's friend, then comes the horse,
with others the cat...; but whatever kind
of animal it is a person likes,
it's all hunky-dory so long as there's
a place in the heart for one or a few of them.

WILLIAM JAMES

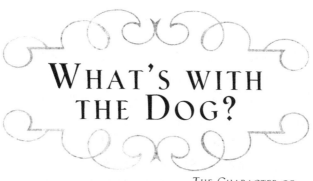

WHAT'S WITH THE DOG?

THE CHARACTER OF

Rich Mullins

My God will meet all *your needs.*

PHILIPPIANS 4:19 (EMPHASIS ADDED)

I was working for a publisher, trying to secure permission to use a music video of the prolific Christian songwriter, Rich Mullins. I had been working on the project for weeks and after numerous phone calls and letters seemed no nearer to securing the needed approval. So I called the record company...again.

"I am approaching the deadline on this project and need to know if we are going to be able to use the video. Can you tell me why the delay?"

A long pause followed my question. I wondered if I was even talking with the right individual until finally I received a response.

"The reason is that Mr. Mullins has to approve the request as well, and we have not been able to reach him."

In a day of cell phones, e-mail, and Global Positioning Systems, I felt the excuse was slightly lame. It's not like this was a last-minute request. Weeks had passed since my initial contact.

"Do you mind me asking why you can't just call him?" I questioned, working to keep the frustration from filtering through my voice. Again, there was a lengthy pause.

"Well, we can't reach him until he contacts us. You see, he is out camping somewhere in his pickup with his dog."

I started to laugh. "You're kidding me, right?"

The silence on the other end let me know that she wasn't. I finally did receive the needed permission, but now I was intrigued.

I went home that night and searched through my music collection, finally reaching the object of my search. On the front of one of Mullins' early albums, *Winds of Heaven, Stuff of Earth,* was...the dog, a beautiful golden lab pictured with Rich that almost received more prominent positioning than Mullins himself. But anyone who knew anything about the anointed songwriter knew that having the spotlight fixed on him was one of the last things he wanted.

While I realize the term "puppy love" is typically referential to infatuation, at least in this book I mean it in its literal sense. Talk to any animal lover and they will let you know their pet is not just a pet, but part of the family. That was certainly true in Mullins' case, as he would often take his dog with him on tour, no small matter for his recording company who had to locate hotels to accommodate his four-legged companion.

As we walk through the seasons of love, our journey wouldn't be complete without some heartwarming stories about man's best friend. And, do dogs go to Heaven? Well, I'm not even opening that can of worms.

Heavenly Father, thank You for the blessing that pets provide. Like You, they love unconditionally and provide warm companionship. Thank You for caring enough about me that You have provided for me even on this basic level. Amen.

RICH MULLINS was killed on September 19, 1997, en route to one of his concerts. His untimely death left behind a legacy of songs that spoke of his faith in God and his desire to live in such a way as to bring glory to the God he served.

At the time of his death, Mullins' family created the nonprofit organization, The Legacy of a Kid Brother of St. Frank, to continue the work Rich had begun, teaching the arts and the love of God to Native American tribes. The organization exists to provide opportunities to develop skills in music, fine art, literature, and other artistic pursuits, following the example set by Saint Francis. For additional information contact:

The Legacy of a Kid Brother of St. Frank, P. O. Box 11526, Wichita, KS 67202; or call (316) 262-7159.

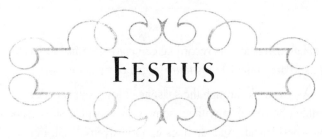

FESTUS

God made all sorts of wild animals, livestock,
and small animals, each able to reproduce more
of its own kind. And God saw that it was good.

GENESIS 1:25 NLT

Festus wasn't your typical dog, but that was fitting since the Schieles weren't your typical family. Festus was a purebred Russian Golden Retriever—a dog with a history shrouded in drama. According to legend, Scotsman Sir Dudley Majoribanks, later known as Lord Tweedmouth, was visiting the English seaside town of Brighton. During his visit, he attended a traveling circus and was captivated by a troupe of performing Russian sheepdogs. After the performance he approached the dogs' trainer, endeavoring to purchase a pair of the dogs; however, the owner refused, unwilling to break up the troupe. As the story goes, in the end Tweedmouth is said to have purchased the entire lot. He then took them back to Scotland and bred them as what is known today as the Russian golden retriever—a breed well-known for its loyalty and gentle demeanor.

Festus was gentle all right—and stubborn and protective and mammoth in size, a dog lovingly referred to as "just a big ole teddy bear." But I'm getting ahead of the story.

According to his papers, the small golden ball of fur was born to a professional breeder, who first named him Tanner. Interestingly, it was this breeder's custom to give one pup from each litter as an "offering" to a deserving family. The Schieles were the blessed recipients, an answer to prayer for Scott who had owned a golden retriever as a boy and wanted the same experience for his own family.

Once the dog came to live with Scott, his wife, Marla, and their three children, "Tanner" was quickly dropped and replaced with what seemed a more fitting name—Festus. After all, the Schieles already had a dog named Dillon and a cat named Miss Kitty, and Festus just fit right in. But unlike his namesake from the long-running western television series, Festus the dog was more than able to handle any situation. In fact, he thought he could do anything, and he almost could.

The Schieles hadn't owned Festus long when Scott relocated to a new position as director of a large church camp in rural Oklahoma. Their home now on the campgrounds, Festus had more than ten acres on which to roam and soon became the self-proclaimed king of the property. And he let everyone know it.

Even as a small pup, Festus learned that possums and skunks were undesirable critters. The trailer the Schieles lived in upon their arrival seemed to attract the possums, which would often climb up into the insulation in the trailer and suffocate. The stench of the carcasses would permeate every inch of the trailer until Scott could locate the source of the offensive odor. Unfortunately, locating the dead animals wasn't all that easy.

Festus soon solved the dilemma as he quickly learned to notify Scott when the possums or skunks drew near the trailer. As Festus grew to the size of a miniature horse, the varmints stayed away from the camp and ceased to be a problem. Scott never again had to worry about losing his chickens to foxes or chasing off skunks. Festus was officially on the throne. Well, almost. As the young, headstrong dog grew in size, he decided to test his authority. He seemed to be aware of his dominating presence and rather enjoyed it.

At only two years old, Festus had reached a daunting ninety-five pounds. And even at that early age, he didn't just walk around the camp, he sauntered, having well established that the campground was *his* turf. And then one day—he disappeared.

Festus was gone for two days, leaving no clue as to his whereabouts. It wasn't like him to wander off and the Schieles feared the worst. On the third day, however, Scott looked up and noticed Festus limping slowly down the graveled road to the house. "From a distance he looked as if he had been hit by a car," Scott remembers of that day long ago.

"When I got to him, I saw that he had been injured in several places. A huge chunk had been taken out of one of his legs, and there were gashes and cuts all along his body. I immediately called the vet, describing as best I could the extent of Festus' injuries.

"'I can't do anything for him," the vet explained. 'It sounds like he met up with a pack of coyotes and more than likely tried to take over the harem. If he's alive by tomorrow, he might make it.'"

Amazingly, Festus did recover. But it wasn't clear whether or not the incident had done anything to take his ego down a notch. From the time Festus had come to live with them, Scott had worked with the dog, using hand signals to dictate various commands. Without a word Scott could communicate to the oversized dog to sit, stay, and lie down. But Festus' maturity didn't match his size. Like a young child, he complied to the latter command, but often with only partial obedience. When instructed to lie down, he would usually respond, but ever so slowly, leaving his backside hiked in the air. His protest seemed to imply, "I'll obey, but you can't make me lie down all the way." After he had made his point, he would finally defer to his master's insistence.

If Scott was in charge, then Festus was his undisputed next in command when it came to the camp. Even Marla, Scott's wife, knew that when her husband was gone, Festus ruled the roost. But no one seemed to complain, because it was well understood that Festus would protect them all.

Late one evening, after the Schieles had gone to bed, Festus began barking incessantly. Scott and Marla listened as the sound headed off into the distance, coming from somewhere behind the trailer. Scott had learned from experience that Festus didn't bark without a reason, so he quickly grabbed his flashlight to take a look around. Walking out to the area where he thought he had heard the dog, he searched for a few moments, but saw and heard nothing. Eventually he returned to bed.

But the next morning, in the full light of day, Scott could read the story of the previous night as clearly as if he were reading a newspaper. He first noticed a vacancy in the stand of canoes where one boat was now missing. Following a path about a hundred yards, Scott saw the stolen canoe where it had been dropped. Footprints leading away from the stand were of two people taking small measured steps, evidence that the thieves worked together to carry off the sixteen-foot, twelve-hundred-dollar canoe. But where the canoe had been dropped, the footsteps parted in opposite directions, leaving behind a trail of prints with great strides between them. It wouldn't be the last time Festus protected the camp from theft.

As fierce as Festus had proven to be with the intruders, he proved as loving and tender to the young campers who came each summer. Festus had an uncanny way of picking out the child in each group who seemed most insecure in the new surroundings and stuck to the youngster like glue. The presence of such a cuddly new friend not only gave the insecure camper confidence, it also created an instant rapport with all the other children vying for Festus' attention. When campers returned the following year, Scott and Marla would stand at the lodge to greet the children, who usually ran right past them in their haste to reunite with their most beloved member of the staff...Festus.

Such rapport wasn't without cost; Festus came to expect the constant attention of the campers and wouldn't be denied even when their focus seemed to shift. It was common for Festus to walk up to be petted and lean heavily into the individual until he received his due. Completely relaxing in the moment, on more than one occasion Festus actually fell over when the person started to walk away.

One of the Schiele's favorite stories is of a time when an older gentleman was visiting the camp. For hours the fisherman had tried to hook a prize from the stocked pond with no success. Finally, Festus sidled up to where the fisherman stood, walked into the pond, and pulled out a fish with his mouth. Triumphant, he looked at the fisherman as if to say, "See, that's how you do it."

Festus had been part of the Schiele family for ten years when Scott noticed that something wasn't quite right. Oh, Festus could still run faster than anything or anybody at the camp, that is once he got to his feet, but when Scott looked into his eyes, something wasn't quite right. He just couldn't put his finger on it.

Then one overcast morning in the hot summer, Scott received a call from the camp cook. "I think Festus has died. He's all curled up in front of the lodge, and he hasn't moved at all."

Scott arrived only to confirm the cook's suspicion, the dog's body already stiff. As the clouds gathered, Scott started the dreaded task of preparing for the burial. Too heavy to lift, Scott scooped Festus up with the tractor and headed to the makeshift burial site by the lake. Several times during the task, Scott looked up to see their other dog, Dillon, standing atop the hill.

Typically, Dillon would have been at Scott's heels, joining in whatever project was at hand. But not today. Dillon kept his distance throughout the entire process, seeming to reverence the final moments that his master had with the beloved Festus.

Just as Scott finished covering the newly dug grave, the pregnant clouds burst forth, soaking him through within minutes. The weather fit his mood as he drove the tractor back to the shed, water streaming down his cheeks from more than just rain.

It's been almost a year since Festus' death. Summer has returned and so have the young campers. Actually so have all the critters as well—the possums, the skunks, and even a pack of stray dogs who killed every one of the Schiele's chickens while Dillon stood and watched.

"Dillon didn't have a clue as to what to do when it happened," Marla explains. "He had never learned because Festus always took care of it. Festus took care of everything."

Dear God, life can be bittersweet. The gift of a pet enriches life, the animal becoming one of the family. And just as the death of a loved one leaves an empty spot, which no other person can fill, the death of a pet leaves a void too. Other pets may come and go, but not one can take the place of another. Thank You for such precious gifts. Amen.

How a Donkey Saved My Life

A righteous man cares for the needs of his animal.

PROVERBS 12:10

The heat of the noonday sun beat upon the middle-aged Arab as he guided his donkey along the dusty, well-worn trail. The two were as familiar with this path as with each other, having traveled the route between the two cities numerous times over the years. This time Balaam and his faithful beast were accompanied by two of Balaam's servants and distinguished princes who had been sent by the king of Moab. Balaam hoped to redeem himself in their eyes.

For the first several hours as they plodded along in silence, he replayed the events of the previous day in his mind. Anger didn't even begin to describe his emotions as he relived the events over again—what he had wanted to do, what he should have said. Almost from the beginning, his audience before the king had gone horribly awry. His hopes of wealth and esteem, which had seemed imminent when the king summoned for his counsel, were now slipping through his fingers like grains of sand.

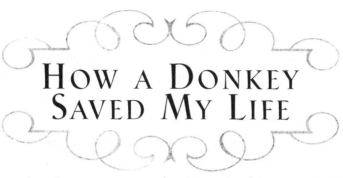

He cursed aloud as the sweat trickled down his face and back, forming a thin layer of muck as the grit from the dirt road now stuck to him like glue. He cursed again, kicking the animal underneath him.

As they continued on their way, Balaam spoke aloud, "Blasted, no–good beast. Move!" This was the second time that day that the stubborn animal wouldn't cooperate, this time crushing his master's foot against one of the walls on either side of the path. He raised his whip and released the frustration from his failed negotiations onto the back of the animal.

"I should kill you for your insolence," he fumed, rubbing his injured foot as the animal finally eased back into the center of the rugged path.

As they neared the city, the dusty trail began to narrow, turning the path into little more than an enclosed foot trail. It would be a tight fit as he maneuvered his donkey onward. However, instead of proceeding, the animal lay down, his master still seated atop his back.

Balaam raised his hand to strike the beast again when he heard the rebuke, "What have I done to you to make you beat me these three times?"

Without hesitation Balaam answered the donkey, as if a conversation with his beast were commonplace.

"You have made a fool of me! If I had a sword in my hand, I would kill you right now."

The donkey replied to Balaam, "Am I not the same donkey you've ridden every day? Have I been in the habit of doing this to you?"

"No," he said.

Instantly Balaam's eyes were opened and he saw the angel of the Lord directly in front of him, sword raised. With that, the angel chastised Balaam for his wickedness.

In disobedience to God, Balaam had stubbornly set off on this journey in hopes of obtaining the wealth and acclaim from the king that he so desired. If it hadn't been for his faithful donkey, he might well have lost his life.[1]

The next time you find yourself behaving as "stubborn as a mule," why not let a word to the wise be sufficient. When God says no, be willing to let it go. It could keep you from looking like a fool—or worse.

LIFE LESSONS

1. Day-to-day life can get frustrating. Use caution how, where, and to whom you vent your anger.
2. Willingness to override moral integrity for wealth and prestige will eventually lead to disaster.
3. Faithful obedience to God's direction leads to the King's reward.

---

[1] Story based upon 2 Peter 2:15–16 and Numbers 22.

SECTION 2

Unexpected Friend

A real friend is one who walks in
when the rest of the world walks out.

AUTHOR UNKNOWN

COCKROACH-INSPIRED FRIENDSHIP[2]

Shelley Breen

OF POINT OF GRACE

A friend loves at all times,
and a brother is born for adversity

PROVERBS 17:17

It was my first semester at college, and I hardly knew anyone. I was fast asleep in my little twin bed in my dorm room when I felt something crawling on my leg. Surely I was dreaming. Then, I felt it on my arm, but I couldn't see anything in the bed, so I tried to go back to sleep. And then it happened. Crawling across my face, *yes my face,* was a huge roach!! I sat up, screamed, and flicked it onto the floor. This gave me a case of the heebie-jeebies of the worst kind. And this roach was no small creature; it was more like a bug on major steroids.

---

[2] Excerpted from "Circle of Friends" © 1999 by Point of Grace. Used by permission of Howard Publishing Co., West Monroe, Louisiana. All rights reserved.

Anyhow, I was certain of this one thing: I was *not* spending the rest of the night in my bed.

The only option who came to mind was Cathy Daniel. When she answered her door, her face reflected her bewilderment. I must have looked pathetic, standing there in my jammies and clutching my blanket. "May I sleep in your bed with you tonight?" I explained that a large roach was currently borrowing mine. She kindly consented, but I know she must have been thinking, *Now what's your name?* As I drifted off to sleep in her crowded bed, I thought that surely Cathy and I would become friends for life. And so we have.

God, thanks for the gift of friends. My life would be so colorless without them. Sometimes I need "Jesus with skin on," and often You use my friends to meet that need. Continue to bring new friends into my life, while helping me to nurture my existing relationships. Help me to be a friend whom others can count on. Amen.

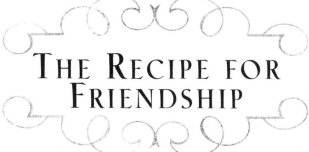

The Recipe for Friendship

Two are better than one,
because they have a good return for their work:
If one falls down, his friend can help him up.

Ecclesiastes 4:9–10

"What do you think?" Regina asked as I began to chew the small white lump she offered from the plate she held in front of me. She leaned closer as I caught sight of her son, Patrick, shaking his head. My taste buds registered their complaint at the same time that my mind registered Patrick's reaction. This wasn't going to be good.

Regina and I had become friends three years earlier after my husband and I moved to the People's Republic of China. We had been hired to teach English in one of their numerous universities in northeast China. Regina was one of three native English teachers already employed by the university. Her command of the English language was very good, and we quickly became close friends in spite of our cultural differences.

Regina was an amazing cook. We spent hours together as she taught me the art of Chinese cooking. I, in turn, taught her how to bake in one of the small countertop ovens (that were not much bigger than a Mattel Easy Bake oven) that had recently become available in their state-run stores. While learning to blend the right spices for the dishes we shared, our lives also mingled during our long talks and shared experiences. It was an unusual friendship that I treasured more each day.

My taste buds were now in full complaince from Regina's latest culinary attempt. One thing was certain. This was no cookie!

"Mom, they don't taste like Karen's," commented Patrick as he looked at me with a pained look in his eyes. I noticed belatedly that *he* wasn't eating her cookies. Neither was her husband. All three stared at me as I continued to chew. The crumbly concoction stuck in my throat as my mind raced for something kind to say.

"What did you put in them?" I asked, stalling.

"Well, I followed the recipe," she began, "except I cut out two-thirds of the sugar and substituted pig lard for the butter. Oh, and I didn't think it really needed two eggs, so I only added one," she concluded. Her practical and conservative Chinese upbringing made it difficult for Regina to follow what seemed to her an extravagant use of ingredients.

Our approach to cooking mirrored the vast cultural differences of our lives, yet somehow in spite of the gulf between us, a bridge was built as we shared not only our recipes, but our lives.

When I gave birth to my first child in a Chinese hospital a couple of years later, it was Regina who stood with my husband and me, holding my hand and offering words of encouragement. A few months later when her mother-in-law passed away unexpectedly, I offered her a shoulder to cry on and prayers for support.

As I look back over our friendship, I realize how easily it could have been lost. Differences in language, in culture, in lifestyle. How much we miss when we build friendships only with those like ourselves.

In a land far away, I found that the ingredients for a lasting friendship—love, acceptance, and understanding—are always the same and always yield rewarding results when we are careful to follow the recipe.

Father, thank You for all the wonderful things friendships bring to my life. Help my friends and me to celebrate each other's strengths and encourage one another in our weaknesses. I celebrate the uniqueness of each individual You bring across my path because each represents a facet of You. I recognize that variety really is the spice of life. Amen.

Grandma Hester

Jenni's Story

Encourage each other and build each other up,
just as you are already doing.

1 Thessalonians 5:11 NLT

It was an unlikely friendship birthed out of unexpected circumstances. Ironically, their relationship lasted only a week, but it marked Jenni's heart for life.

Up and down the tree-lined street was a hodgepodge of families, from newlyweds to those with young children to the elderly and everything in between. Jenni's family lived next door to a couple in their fifties. Their children grown, the pair kept to themselves for the most part. The only thing about them that really captured ten-year-old Jenni's attention was their beautiful black and white German shepherd who playfully licked her fingers each time she tried to pet him over the fence.

When her neighbors planned to leave for a week's vacation, they asked Jenni to feed and water the dog in their absence and offered to pay her for her effort. Well, it didn't take much consideration before Jenni happily agreed.

But *pay* her to feed and play with their dog? Puzzled, Jenni just shook her head.

The next morning around 7:00, Jenni headed next door. Locating the dog's bowl, she was surprised to discover it was completely full. *Why hasn't he eaten his food?* she wondered. Having a dog of her own, Jenni pondered the possibilities, the most obvious being either illness or sadness at the absence of his owners. Concerned, she patted the big dog as he playfully dropped his stick in front of her. His entire body swayed back and forth from his rapidly wagging tail. He sure didn't *seem* to be upset.

After refilling the water bowl, Jenni picked up the stick and tossed it across the yard. In the next instant, the dog whizzed past in close pursuit. They continued their game for several minutes until Jenni heard the sliding glass door on the back of the house open. She quickly spun around, every sound and movement now magnified. The house was supposed to be empty.

"Won't you come in for a moment?" asked the petite white-haired woman standing in the doorway. "I'm Fred's mother."

The woman seemed harmless enough, but Jenni's heart was still racing as she nodded her consent. Patting the dog for reassurance, Jennie headed inside.

As Jenni recalls that day, she shares, "I didn't know what to say, uncertain if I should even be in the house. But before I could retreat, Grandma Hester, as she introduced herself, took my hand and led me into the kitchen."

"I already fed the dog this morning. She seemed hungry," Grandma Hester said, which explained the mystery of the full bowl of food. "Would you like some breakfast? I was just fixing some eggs and toast."

Jenni perched on the tall stool, still uncertain about what to do. She wasn't at all sure her neighbors would appreciate her eating their food when, in fact, she was supposed to be out taking care of the dog. But it was too late as "Grandma" placed a glass of cold milk and a slice of buttered toast in front of her. As she cracked an egg into the hot skillet, Grandma Hester chatted of this and that, keeping up a steady conversation until Jenni realized they had eaten everything. Glancing at the clock over the table, her eyes widened. It had been well over an hour since she had left to feed the dog. Worried that her mother would wonder where she was, she quickly excused herself, checking the dog as she went out the back door.

Guilt weighed on Jenni's young shoulders the remainder of the day.

"My neighbors were paying me to do what? Certainly not eat their food," Jenni shares. "I determined to get up even earlier the next morning, so Grandma Hester wouldn't have to do my job for me."

The next morning Jenni headed for her assigned task an hour earlier than the previous morning. But once again, she found the dog's bowl completely full and the patio wet from the refilling of the water bowl. She began to play with the dog, until she heard the glass door slide open in what was to become a familiar pattern as Grandma Hester invited her to breakfast.

Over the next five days, the routine was the same. No matter how early Jenni arrived, Grandma Hester had already fed the dog, but was ready for her breakfast companion. Each morning over eggs, toast, and milk, Grandma shared of days gone by. Then somehow she would get the shy young girl, who needed someone to listen, to talk about her school and friends, offering a sympathetic ear or some measure of advice. Their morning talks grew longer with each day until the week was over. With regret, Jenni noted that her neighbors would return from vacation the following day.

"Arriving home, they immediately came to pay me for feeding the dog. I felt guilty accepting the money, knowing I had done so little," Jenni remembers.

At ten years old, it was difficult to process the realities of the grown-up world. However, now grown with a family of her own, Jenni realizes the truth of what really transpired that special week.

"More than just taking care of their dog, our neighbor recognized his mother's need for companionship. I had done my job; I just hadn't known it at the time," Jenni reflects.

Jenni and her family moved not long after, and she never saw Grandma Hester again.

"Well into her eighties at that time, I often wondered how she was and if she were still alive," Jenni finishes. "But I will always treasure the unlikely friendship between that shy young girl and a sweet eighty-year-old woman who both just needed someone to talk to."

Heavenly Father, help me to be sensitive to the needs of others. In my busyness, it is easy to rush through life and miss out on the pleasure of stopping to chat now and then. Help me to be sensitive to the people I come in contact with, and remind me to take time for what is really important. Amen.

He Can't Be Trusted

Jesus said, "If your brother sins, rebuke him, and if he repents, forgive him. If he sins against you seven times in a day, and seven times comes back to you and says, 'I repent,' forgive him."

LUKE 17:3–4

"I won't have him," Paul insisted. "Just when we needed him most, he abandoned us. You have to understand, Barnabas, your cousin's immaturity is not just a frustration; it can be dangerous to our cause."

Barnabas fought to hide the smile that threatened as Paul continued to rail against John Mark. It hadn't been too many years before when Paul had been in a position similar to that of the young protégé. Yet recognizing the great potential in him, Barnabas and the other disciples had patiently guided and admonished him. These thoughts went unspoken, however, as Barnabas continued to try to persuade his friend and counterpart.

"He's a good man, Paul. He has grown significantly, and I know that he will be helpful to us," Barnabas countered. "Let's just give him another chance."

But Paul remained unbending. He may have forgiven John Mark, but he refused to forget. Finally, the disagreement reached an impasse, as neither man was willing to concede to the other. So the two friends went their separate ways to continue their work apart.

Details are scarce regarding the ongoing work of Barnabas and John Mark as they headed to Cyprus and other regions. In fact, years passed before Mark was even mentioned again. Ironically, though, almost seventeen years later, after imprisonment and the desertion of another fellow worker, Paul wrote to his friends for assistance: "Only Luke is with me. Get [John] Mark and bring him with you, because he is helpful to me in my ministry."

Under the mentoring guidance of his cousin Barnabas, John Mark reached a level of maturity that benefited the church. And when Paul was finally able to acknowledge the growth and change, John Mark provided him with the assistance and friendship sorely needed in the latter years of his ministry—an unexpected, but God-given friend.[3]

LIFE LESSONS

1. Friends are a gift from God, and He can bring them into your life at the most unexpected times and in unusual places. Be mindful of the new people who cross your path. God may use you to be the "gift" they need that day.

[3] Story based upon Acts 15:37–40 and 2 Timothy 4:11.

2. Don't let offenses rob you of special relationships.
3. To have friends you must learn to be a friend. Make the decision to be a blessing to others.

SECTION 3

Best Friends

Everyone hears what you say.

Friends listen to what you say.

Best friends listen to what you don't say.

AUTHOR UNKNOWN

THE BLESSINGS OF FRIENDSHIP[4]

Barbara Johnson

I am a friend to all who fear you,
to all who follow your precepts.

PSALM 119:63

It has been said that there is inexpressible comfort in being able to feel safe with a friend—not having to weigh thoughts or measure words, but being allowed to pour them all right out, just as they are, chaff and grain together, knowing that she will keep what is worth keeping and, with a breath of kindness, blow the rest away.

What a blessing to have friends with whom to share our joys and our sorrows. When sorrow is shared, it is divided, and when joy is shared it is multiplied. One truth I have enjoyed sharing is that *openness is to wholeness* what *secrets are to sickness.*

---

[4] Excerpted from *Circle of Friends* © 1999 by Point of Grace. Used by permission of Howard Publishing Co., West Monroe, Louisiana. All rights reserved.

The full meaning of this is that we can become well by sharing our pain with a friend who can keep confidences and be understanding. A sense of wholeness and well-being results when we are able to unburden ourselves with a trusted friend.

This is how our fellowship with Christ can be. He knows our every need; He knows our limitations and our faults. What a comfort to know that when we confess our sins and receive His forgiveness, God no longer sees our sins because they are removed as far as the east is from the west.

A friend is someone who understands your past, believes in your future, and accepts you just the way you are. I've heard sympathy defined as "your pain in my heart." How true that sharing our pain with our friends binds us so close to them that we experience their sorrow as our own. What a luxury it is to have friends who take our pain into their hearts. Through Christ, we have such a circle of friends.

Heavenly Father, I treasure the friends You have given me, friends who are there when I need them—to listen, encourage, and believe in me. It is comforting when they share my pain and exhilarating when they share my joy. Help me to be the friend they need as well. Above all, O God, I praise You for being the ultimate friend to me. I love You. Amen.

Green Light Bulbs

But there is a friend who sticks closer than a brother.

Proverbs 18:24 NKJV

It was a typical Sunday morning mingling with friends before the service began. Although taking place in church, what happened next was the stuff of soap operas.

I turned from talking with one gal and headed over to the bench where a pretty girl was engaged in conversation with a cute blond guy. In the next moment, I noticed they were holding hands. The only problem was, the cute girl was my best friend while the hand she was holding was that of—my boyfriend...or so I thought. For most friendships, that would have signaled the end, but not ours. You see, we were only three years old at the time. That was more than thirty-five years ago.

A memorable birthday card that I received not long ago spoke of a lasting friendship. On the front, Winnie-the-Pooh is talking to his dear friend Piglet, and he says, "If you live to be a hundred, I want to live to be a hundred minus one day, so I never have to live without you." A sweet sentiment to be sure; unfortunately, the reality of our lives today is that few friendships survive any real length of time.

A few years ago, I worked in the human resources department of a small company. I was amazed at the number of résumés that crossed my desk listing personal references of relationships only two to three years old. Rarely listed were mature relationships of more than ten years. Did these individuals not possess friendships that had stood the test of time? No wonder the divorce rate in our country is so high, when even platonic friendships flow in and out of our lives and can be discarded as easily as an empty sack.

The art of friendship is often forgotten in our society of instant gratification. Friendships take time and the best ones, like soup on a cold winter's day, have simmered slowly over a long period of time, creating a distinct flavor that only the shared experiences of joy and pain can bring.

Linda is one such friend. The hand-holding moment with the cute blond was quickly forgiven and forgotten. He disappeared from our friendship as numerous boyfriends would over the years. We have shared the joys of birthdays, getting our driver's licenses, graduation, college, new jobs, marriage, and the birth of my children. We have also been there for each other through the pain of failed tests, broken relationships, deaths in the family, and now caring for our aging parents.

Growing up, I was the shorthaired tomboy who spoke too loud and too often. She was the more graceful beauty with flowing long brown hair and a gentle demeanor. But put us together and the combination became electric, somehow balancing our differences. It was not uncommon for teachers to confuse our names, sending the class into a fit of laughter. Rarely was there one of us without the other. The dynamic duo we were—at least in our minds—ready to save the world.

As the years progressed, we would often finish each other's sentences, knowing from experience the likes, dislikes, and thought processes of the other. One such memorable instance was our journey to shop for the perfect wedding gift for a mutual friend. We walked the aisles together, picking up and setting aside numerous items. Too expensive, too cheap, too tacky. We laughed and talked, just enjoying the adventure and being together.

Turning down yet another aisle, suddenly we found ourselves out of the housewares department. In fact, it hardly looked like we were even in the same store. A strange assortment of odds and ends now stretched before us, piled in baskets of varying shapes and sizes. We were definitely on the wrong aisle.

"Well, what would work for a wedding gift here?" I laughed, shaking my head as my eyes took in a basket of wooden nickels next to a case of rat traps. There were small, round, metal thing-a-ma-jigs beside some large wooden doo-dads. It was impossible to tell what some of these items were supposed to be. Our attempt at humor was now in full swing and escalating as we joked about the feasibility of any of the items serving as a wedding gift. Our minds knew no limit as the easy flow of our friendship gave full vent to our "creative" imaginings.

And then, as if one, our eyes landed on a huge bin as we exclaimed in unison, "Green light bulbs!"

As we fixated on the emerald glass bulbs—and not the Christmas light variety—I didn't have to guess why they still had such an enormous supply. It also made me wonder who had received the appropriate tongue-lashing for the ridiculous purchase. Still giggling from our identical reaction, we discussed possible uses for the light bulbs as a wedding gift, which only increased our mirth. It became a defining moment of our friendship that even years later we only have to mention "green light bulbs" to express our mutual mind-set.

"It's scary!" my husband commented once after Linda had come over for a brief visit. More than once during the conversation, Linda and I had passed each other a knowing glance. No words were expressed, yet volumes had been spoken.

Our adventures with mud pies, lemonade stands, long bike rides, and slumber parties are now only memories except for the occasional lunch appointments we share to celebrate birthdays and holidays. Our lives now hold few similarities. I have three small children while she and her husband have chosen not to have kids. My husband and I work in the ministry, while she and her husband own and manage a successful business. Although our lives have taken us in different directions, the substance that holds our friendship together was forged in the fire of commitment long ago.

Due to the busyness and demands of daily life, it would be easy to let this friendship slowly whither away, leaving behind only sweet childhood memories and pictures in dusty photo albums. At times it's easier to start a new friendship than to work at maintaining an existing one through all of life's transitions. It's easier, but not nearly as rewarding.

Although I have made numerous friends over the years, many whom I talk to with greater frequency, it was Linda whom I called first when my father passed away recently. The depth of our friendship transcended the years as she comforted me in my time of grief. She waited with me in silence as the tears came and I could no longer speak. But I had no doubt that she would understand everything, although I could say nothing. After all, we both understood green light bulbs.

God, thank You for the lifelong friends You have given me, who remain precious to me today. It is such a gift to be known and accepted for who I am, and that can only happen over time. Help me to make the effort to continue nurturing these relationships, and help us to encourage one another to continue growing in You. Amen.

FROM MOTHER-IN-LAW TO MOTHER-IN-LOVE

Jill's Story

A wise man's heart guides his mouth,
and his lips promote instruction.

PROVERBS 16:23

"I was really frightened at the prospect of becoming a mother-in-law. When my three sons all married within ten months of each other, I thought, *What am I going to do with girls?* It was all such new territory for me," Jill begins.

Jill faced a common concern as she prepared for the approaching change in her relationship with her three sons and soon-to-be daughters.

Not long after my own wedding, my mother-in-law inserted a similar thought into one of our conversations.

"Karen, I hope we will always get along like we do now," she said, a note of sadness in her voice.

I was surprised by the comment and studied her closely. "Why wouldn't we?" I asked, surprised. From the time I met them, I liked my husband's parents and there was an easy rapport between us. I couldn't imagine it ever being any different.

"Well, you often hear of disagreements between mothers-in-law and daughters-in-law. I don't want that to ever happen to us," she confided.

"It won't if we don't let it," I assured her. And it hasn't. Now almost fifteen years later, we still have a strong and loving relationship. A friendship.

As the first wedding date approached, Jill continued to pray for wisdom.

"The first thing God showed me was to back off. Once our children are grown, our position in their lives changes. We are no longer trainers, but advisors. My husband, Ron, and I determined that we wouldn't offer advice unless they first asked for it. That means even when we see them making what we feel are erroneous decisions. However, because we determined to do this, our sons and daughters-in-law often do ask our opinion. It doesn't mean they always take our advice, but they always listen and are appreciative.

"I also determined to be available to my new daughters whether that meant helping to baby-sit, going swimming, shopping, or just talking. This has allowed our relationships to develop to a place of acceptance and trust. In fact, all three girls and I recently took a trip to Dallas to go shopping. We truly enjoyed our growing friendship and just being together.

"As we have worked to create strong relationships within our family, my husband and I have chosen to be open with them regarding difficulties we have faced in our own marriage in hopes that they can learn from our mistakes and avoid the same pitfalls.

"Finally, we made the decision to give. As holidays approach, we realize it can be stressful for young married couples as they struggle to fit everyone into their holiday schedule. Because we live in the same city as all three of our children, we have the opportunity to see them on a regular basis. So we have let them know that during holidays they can feel free to spend those days with other family members. We simply move our celebration with them to another day. It's not the day that matters, but the time together."

The result for Jill and her extended family from all of these practices has been obvious as the relationships have blossomed and developed a firm foundation of trust and communication.

"As far as my daughters-in-law, I couldn't feel closer to these three lovely ladies if they were my own flesh-and-blood daughters," Jill says.

"I have learned over the years that the most important thing I can do is to keep my mouth shut. And in that case, less is definitely more."

Dear God, being an in-law—whether a mother- or father-in-law, or a son- or daughter-in-law—can be tricky. I need Your wisdom to fulfill this role well. Help me be quick to hear and slow to speak—to offer advice only when it is asked for, to humbly receive encouraging words when they are given. Help me to be respectful of my in-laws at all times. May I be a blessing to them and love them the way that You do. Amen.

STRONGER THAN DEATH

The LORD will watch us both while we are apart from each other.

GENESIS 31:49 CEV

My own father tried to kill me...

The thought pounded in his brain as Jonathan and his servant made their way to the field at the edge of the city. Realization washed over him as the long-ignored signs came rolling through his mind with vivid clarity. The eruptions of anger; the plotting; and now by his father's own admittance, attempted murder. When he couldn't reach the object of his murderous jealousy, the fevered pitch of his outrage lashed out at his own son.

*My father's insane...*Jonathan finally admitted to himself as he slid off his horse at the appointed rendezvous, grabbing the pouch of slender arrows.

"Run," Jonathan called to the young lad. "It's further beyond you. Run, don't delay." In obedience, the young boy ran to retrieve the arrows that had been shot across the field, while at the sound of the code, a shadowy figure emerged from the nearby forest.

The two men stood in the grassy field overlooking the city. They had come there often to practice, always ending in a friendly competition of who could out do the other. But this time a gripping silence hung between them in the early morning light. This time the stakes were a matter of life and death.

"You were right," Jonathan finally spoke, his voice shaking with anger. "My father became enraged when he found out you were gone. He fears that you hold the hearts of the people and with it the future of the kingdom...my family's kingdom.

"You will be king, David," Jonathan spoke out prophetically to his closest friend, "and I will work alongside you." There was no animosity in his voice toward the man who would ultimately supersede him as the future king, only an acknowledgement of God's plan and the reinforcement of their covenant of friendship.

"May the Lord be with you as he has been with my father. But show me unfailing kindness like that of the Lord as long as I live, so that I may not be killed, and do not ever cut off your kindness from my family,"[5] Jonathan continued.

David and Jonathan embraced as David prepared to leave on a journey that would take him away from Saul and through a maturing process that would ultimately lead him to take the

[5] 1 Samuel 20:13–15.

throne. He would be remembered as one of the greatest kings in the history of Israel.

The depth of the relationship between Jonathan and David provides a rare glimpse into true covenant friendship, two lives bound together with a verbal oath to protect one another as well as their posterity. The strength of this bond is found not only in Jonathan's willingness to relinquish his crown to David, but later, after Jonathan's death, when David spared the life of Jonathan's only remaining son, Mephibosheth.

Their covenant remained in death as it had been in life with Jonathan's final words to his friend, "Go in peace, for we have sworn friendship with each other in the name of the Lord, saying, 'The Lord is witness between you and me, and between your descendants and my descendants forever'" (1 Sam. 20:42). [6]

LIFE LESSONS

1. A true friend rejoices even when his friend's success supersedes his own.
2. The foundation of true friendship is not based upon close proximity or position, but upon a decision of the heart.
3. Friendship, as in any relationship, requires sacrifice. Without that commitment, it is simply a relationship of convenience.

[6] Story based upon 1 Samuel 20 and 2 Samuel 9.

Romantic Love

Two souls with but a single thought,
Two hearts that beat as one.

Maria Lovell

SECTION 4

Love at First Sight

Once in a while,
Right in the middle of an ordinary life,
Love gives us a fairy tale.
AUTHOR UNKNOWN

I Wasn't Looking for a Wife

Michael W. Smith

You have ravished my heart, my lovely one, my bride;
I am overcome by one glance of your eyes.

Song of Solomon 4:9 TLB

"I had no intention of getting married," says award-winning songwriter, Michael W. Smith. "[Debbie] just walked past me, and all of a sudden my life changed. I had seen her maybe three seconds and had fallen in love."[7]

Prior to that life-changing moment, Smith was finally seeing his dream of a career in music come alive. Having written his first song at the tender age of five, his musical passion had already begun to bud. After high school, he enrolled in a university in West Virginia, but dropped out after only one semester to pursue a music career in Nashville. By 1979, having

---

[7] See http://web.archive.org/web/19971210170209/www.ccmcom.com/ccmmag/95sept/smitty.html. Accessed July 30, 2004.

turned his life back to Christ, he made the decision to quit the band he had been traveling with to join a Christian group that needed a keyboard player. It was a decision that would set him on God's path as he literally walked away from his old life, putting out his last cigarette as he went into the audition for the group Higher Ground. For the next year, he traveled with them as their keyboardist until at the age of twenty-four, he was offered his first songwriting contract with Paragon/Benson Publishing Company.

"I thought I'd died and gone to Heaven. I was knocking down $200 a week to do something that I loved. Writing songs for a living meant that I didn't have to wait tables anymore, or work at Coca-Cola, or plant shrubs with a landscaping company.

"I thought my life had peaked and God didn't have to do anything else for me. I wasn't looking for a record deal, a higher salary, or even a girlfriend—and especially not a wife. Writing music, I was as content as I'd ever been, and I labored at it sixteen hours a day. Then one afternoon while I was working in my office, Deborah Kay Davis walked by.

"I thought she was the most beautiful woman I had ever seen. When she passed by, it was all over for me. I was blown away. Totally head over heels in love. I frantically picked up the phone and called my mother in West Virginia.

"'Mom, I can't believe it. You're not going to believe this, Mom. I just saw the girl I'm going to marry.'

"'What's her name?'

"'I don't know, Mom. I haven't met her yet. But I gotta go. I'll find out and call you back.'

"My poor mother! She must have thought I'd lost my mind. But I'd never been so clearheaded in my life.

"I left my office and went searching for this girl in the warehouse. Sherlock Holmes couldn't have done a better job of tracking her down, and eventually I found myself standing outside the ladies' restroom, waiting for her to emerge. She walked out. I introduced myself. We were engaged three and a half weeks later."[8]

The couple's wedding in September 1981—a mere five months after that initial sighting—emphasized just how much the Smiths recognized the hand of God on their lives. "We just felt like God was going to use us in a powerful way to be a light to the world," says Michael.

It was the beginning of a remarkable union that has now lasted almost twenty-five years and still going strong.

God, You are awesome! And You can bring people together any way that You want. I trust You to lead me and guide me every day, to bring those people into my life that You've ordained. Help me to hear Your voice and to know Your will regarding each of them. Amen.

[8] www.michaelwsmith.com/facts/biography.php. Accessed June 2004.

I Was a German War Bride

Charlotte's Story

If anyone is in Christ, he is a new creation;
the old has gone, the new has come!

2 CORINTHIANS 5:17

The American soldiers had just broken through the ranks and were now occupying the area as Hitler's regime of terror finally crumbled. Charlotte and her mother didn't know whether to be grateful or fearful with the presence of these foreign soldiers who were now present among them.

And then one day out of the blue, her best friend asked her a surprising question, "Do you think you could date an American?"

"I don't know," Charlotte replied.

"At the time I didn't know what my feelings were toward these soldiers who now surrounded us," she shares today.

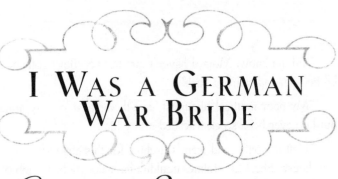

Charlotte was only nine or ten when the war started. Gradually over the next few months, everything Jewish was demolished. She watched helplessly as many were beaten. Several friends from school as well as her own uncle and a grandmother were labeled with the yellow Star of David. Then one day all of the stars simply disappeared. Her uncle never returned from the concentration camps where the Jews were herded.

"I learned to hate at an early age," Charlotte recalls, thinking back to that difficult era. "I hated the man who was responsible for all the destruction that caused my mother and me to flee from city to city. We had to in order to escape from both the ravaging destruction around us and those who sought her for helping the Jews escape."

Charlotte and her mother found themselves in Frankfurt at the end of the war, working as best they could to rebuild their lives. That was when Charlotte's best friend made a surprising announcement.

"I want you to meet my fiancé. His name is Tom...He's an American," she finally added, watching for Charlotte's reaction. Stunned by the revelation, Charlotte didn't realize that there was an even bigger surprise yet to come.

"A few days later, they introduced me to Tom's best friend," she remembers vividly. "Raymond was a handsome young man with the most beautiful green eyes I had ever seen. He was twenty-four and I was fifteen. We fell in love almost immediately, and I became a German war bride."

Shortly after their wedding, Raymond and Charlotte left Germany for a new life in America. But life was not easy.

Charlotte experienced four pregnancies over the next few years that all ended in miscarriages. Her fifth pregnancy finally produced a son. However, Barrett was premature and lived only a short time before they lost him as well.

"My heart was broken," Charlotte shares. "To make matters worse, although I loved my husband, I felt lost and alone in this new culture.

"One night on my way to work, I cried out to God, 'Are You really real? If You are, will You reveal Yourself to me?'"

Driving home alone that night after her work shift, Charlotte struggled to stay awake when suddenly it felt like someone had surrounded her with a warm blanket.

"You *are* real!" she said aloud as the realization of God's presence filled her. As soon as she arrived home, she ran to wake her husband.

"Raymond, Raymond. I'm a Christian!" she said excitedly.

"Oh, is that all," he said as he rolled over and went back to sleep.

Despite her husband's lack of enthusiasm over her life-changing decision, she awoke the next morning realizing that the pain and anger she had carried with her for so long were gone. It was as if she had never seen the sky, the grass, or the trees before; they seemed so indescribably beautiful.

"From that moment on, I couldn't get enough of God," she continues. "Once I started reading the Bible, I just inhaled it. The more I read, the more I felt a release and joy. And I continued to pray for my husband. I knew he believed in God, but I wanted him to know this same joy I had experienced. I attended church and Bible studies by myself until one day, finally, he joined me in the decision to completely turn his life over to Christ."

From that moment on, God began to bless Raymond and Charlotte's home and marriage. In spite of her previous miscarriages, she was able to conceive again; and through prayer, their family began to grow in what had seemed to be an impossible circumstance. They eventually had four healthy children and now have eight grandchildren.

"When I came to America from Germany, I was a young girl with a new husband and a new country. But through God's saving power, now I am a new person."

Dear God, thank You for my mate. I acknowledge You as the Lord of our marriage and that You desire to bless our relationship as we put You first. Remind us to always pray for one another, that together we may fulfill Your plan for our lives. Amen.

Simpler Times, but a Lasting Love

Marie's Story

Many waters cannot quench love,
neither can the floods drown it.

Song of Solomon 8:7 KJV

"It was 1931, and we were in what was called a drought season. The earth was dry and cracked for lack of rain, and the crops were producing very little from their sunburned vines. It was a time when it was normal for families to have seven and eight children, and we all helped in the fields. I was only fifteen that year when I met Elgin and first fell in love," Marie reflects back in time.

"Our family had three boys and four girls. I was only nine when my older sister, Ina, married and moved to Jacksonville, a sister city to where my family lived. After Mama died, I looked forward to the summers when Ina would invite me to spend two or three weeks with her. Those were special times when we would all gather at the church, which served as both a place for community social gatherings as well as a place of worship. It was at one of these gatherings that I first met William Elgin Garrett."

Two years older than Marie, Elgin was of medium build with dark curly hair and a smile that could make you melt. Although her daddy said she was too young to be going out with boys, Elgin always found a seat next to her at the watermelon suppers and afternoon picnics at the church. One of their most memorable outings during that time included a Youth Rally in Little Rock. About seven from their church attended the event.

"Our transportation to the rally had been the back of a big old pickup truck with side rails. We all piled in for the return trip, positioning ourselves near the rails for balance. As we stood, hanging on to the sides, the wind whipped through our hair in the warm summer air as cool drops of rain began to sprinkle on us, eventually turning into a full steady rain. Within minutes we were all soaked, but no one cared. The rain was sorely needed and we were young and carefree."

But the brief rain was not enough to end the drought. Almost all the farming families in the community watched as the little income they had dried up along with their crops. It was about that time that the government developed the Civilian Conservation Camp Program. In those days, the United States was still largely undeveloped and the government was desperately working to build roads. The CC Camp was designed to encourage families to send their young men into the program for a year at a time. In exchange, the family would receive thirty dollars a month and the boys would receive five dollars a month along with their food and a place to sleep. In those desperate times, families worked together. It only made sense for Elgin and his older brother as they signed up for the program. Immediately they left their families and Elgin left Marie.

"Elgin's letters, which came frequently, described the difficult work. The young men used axes and saws to clear roads up through the mountainous regions of Colorado and Utah. With no car and no money for any other form of transportation, there was no way for him to return for a visit for the entire year. But we never complained. He was doing what he had to do as each family member helped carry the load to survive," Marie shares.

"Elgin was eighteen the next time I saw him and more of a man than when he left. He arrived home late on Saturday, and first thing Sunday morning, he walked the eight miles to my house to take me to church. In his hurry to see me, he took a shortcut over a barbed-wire fence and tore his pants! I remember I had to pin his pants before we could go to church that morning. Distance had done nothing to diminish our feelings for one another," Marie laughs.

In no time, the two weeks Elgin was allotted for home leave passed. Before she knew it, Elgin was gone again, starting another one-year contract building roads to provide for his family. That's when the letters grew less and less frequent.

Finally, Marie learned from Elgin's sister that he had met another girl. Eventually the letters stopped altogether.

"About a year later, I met Clayton Dover," Marie shares. "He was a kind man in the community and we married, remaining in the same area as where I had grown up. I heard that Elgin married the other girl and eventually returned to the Arkansas area, settling in Little Rock. Although we lived within twenty minutes of each other, our lives had taken very different directions. It was sixty–two years before our paths crossed again."

After sixteen years of marriage, Marie's first husband passed away, and she remarried to a loving man named Elmer Brannon. From the two marriages, she had seven children.

"Our lives were simple, but compared to the early days of my childhood, we had everything we needed and counted ourselves fortunate. When I became a widow again in 1990, I could look back with a thankful heart at the wonderful marriages and children God had given me. I never dreamed that within a year and a half I would receive a phone call that would completely change my life," Marie continues.

Unknown to Marie, Elgin's wife had also passed away. As his heart healed, he eventually became curious as to what had happened to his first love; and through a mutual friend, he was able to track down her phone number.

"Marie, I would really like to see you again," he started. Hearing his voice brought back memories of years gone by. "Why don't you come to Little Rock and we can meet?" he suggested.

At seventy–four, Marie wasn't about to start chasing any man. "If you want to see me, then you have to come here," Marie told him firmly.

They made a date and met at the local McDonalds. Marie recognized him immediately, although his hair had turned grey and his face was now wrinkled. They drove through the area where Elgin's family had once lived and then to the nearby Air Force base where he had once worked. The conversation came easily and hours passed quickly as the two worked to catch up on the past six decades.

As they parted that evening, Elgin promised to contact Marie again. And he did—as soon as he arrived back home, approximately twenty minutes later!

"He called me every night after that," Marie remembers with a chuckle. "My kids even got on to me, saying they could never get me on the phone because it was always busy!"

About six months later Elgin proposed.

"When I saw you again, it all came back to me how it had been between us. I love you, Marie, and I can't live without you," he said, finally bringing together the love that had started so many years before. It would be a sweet, but short marriage.

Finally together, Marie and Elgin made up for lost time, taking trips together to see autumn foliage and historical sites. At the time of their marriage, Marie was working part time in the local senior's community center. That is until Elgin asked her to quit.

"I just want to spend time with you," he explained. "Time is too short." His words were never truer.

Returning from a routine medical exam three years later, the doctor gave Elgin a clean bill of health. "You're good for another twenty years," the doctor told him as he patted him on the back. Without warning two days later, however, he died from a massive heart attack, leaving Marie a widow once again.

Now in her eighties, Marie has sweet memories. Not of a love that might have been, but of a love that was rekindled when the time was right. It was truly a lasting love.

Father, thank You that Your will is an everlasting will and You bring it to pass at just the right time. It's comforting to know that You work out all things for my good, through thick and thin, the good times and challenging ones. I'm glad I can trust You. Amen.

The Arranged Marriage

He will send his angel before you so that you can get a wife for my son from there.

Genesis 24:7

The day started as every day before it, with very little changing the busy routine of her daily responsibilities. The air was already very warm, with just a hint of the heat that would radiate off the sand by late afternoon. The daughter of a middle-class, Middle Eastern cattleman, Rebekah was like most daughters of that time. Until her family could arrange a suitable marriage that would hopefully bring them honor, her daily task was to water the livestock.

Rebekah was becoming a beautiful woman and possessed a sweet nature. Surely the task of finding the appropriate suitor would not be difficult. But so far their efforts had been unsuccessful. It was almost as if God was preventing every prospect.

As the late afternoon sun gave way to evening and the temperatures began to cool, Rebekah led the family's livestock to the watering hole. Lowering and lifting the heavy jar of water, she repeated the task over and over until the troughs overflowed. As the animals drank, she could finally take a moment to rest and talk with her friends who were performing similar tasks for their families.

Rebekah's attention was suddenly drawn to an approaching stranger. It was obvious he had come a considerable distance. The layer of dust on his beasts and his own garments combined with the weariness on his face were evidence enough. Curious, from behind her veil she took in the details of his clothing. He was well dressed, but a servant; of that she was certain. The ten camels with him were heavy laden with cargo. His eyes surveyed the small group, finally connecting with Rebekah's. She lowered her eyes immediately as the stranger beckoned her.

"Please let down your jar that I may have a drink," he requested.

Immediately Rebekah lowered the heavy jar from her shoulder. As the stranger drank deeply, she was filled with compassion for this weary stranger and his animals.

"I'll draw water for your camels too, until they have drunk their fill," she offered.

Rebekah quickly emptied her jar into the trough and ran back to the well to draw more water, until she had drawn enough for all of his camels. Without saying a word, the man watched her closely. A devout servant, he had been instructed by his aging master to return to the land of his heritage to find a wife for his only son.

"How will I know which is the right one?" the servant questioned.

"God will show you," Abraham instructed with quiet confidence.

Now watching Rebekah as she watered the camels, the servant began to suspect that the Lord had made his journey successful.

When the camels had finished drinking, the man handed Rebekah two golden bracelets. "Whose daughter are you?" he questioned. "Please tell me, is there room in your father's house for us to spend the night?"

As Rebekah revealed her father's name, the servant knew without a doubt that he had found the girl for his master's son. God had led him to his master's relatives!

As she led him to her home, the servant wasted no time in revealing the purpose of his journey.

"It is God's will," Rebekah's father and brother agreed. "We agree to the marriage."

As Rebekah returned with the servant on the long journey back, she wondered of the life that lay before her. Who was this man who would become her husband? It was obvious that he had much wealth. The gifts that the servant had bestowed upon her family testified of that fact. But would he be kind? Would they share love or only children?

As the caravan neared their destination, Rebekah noticed a man walking to meet them.

"Who is that man?" Rebekah questioned the servant.

"He is my master," the servant answered.

History notes that from the first moment, Isaac loved Rebekah. That's not hard to imagine since their marriage had been arranged by God Himself.[9]

LIFE LESSONS

1. Are you single? Have you wondered if you will ever find the right one for you? Be encouraged! When you delight yourself in the Lord, He will order your steps and give you the desires of your heart. (See Psalm 37:4,23.)
2. Every day we are surrounded by miraculous events often disguised in everyday circumstances. Rebekah's kind offer to a complete stranger opened the door to her future as she took the time to help someone in need.
3. Have you been given a task that seems impossible? As Abraham's servant traveled to the distant city, he would have had plenty of time to ponder the very real possibility of failure. As was true for the servant, God has promised to send His angel before us to prepare the way that we should go. You can trust Him.

[9] Story based on Genesis 24.

SECTION 5

True Love

From every human being there rises
a light that reaches straight to Heaven.
And when two souls that are destined to
be together find each other, their streams of
light flow together, and a single brighter light
goes forth from their united being.

AUTHOR UNKNOWN

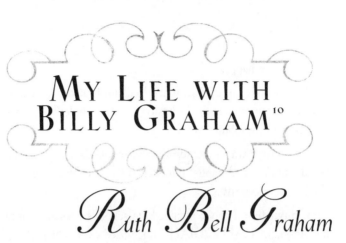

My Life with Billy Graham[10]

Ruth Bell Graham

Follow the way of love.

1 Corinthians 14:1

By 1937, I had my future securely planned. I would never marry. I would spend the rest of my life as a missionary in Tibet. But on July 7 of that year, the Japanese attacked Chinese troops at the Marco Polo Bridge near Beijing, beginning the occupation of northern China. And while my father prepared for war, my mother prepared me for college in the United States. I argued that all I needed was a utilitarian knowledge of Tibetan and the Bible. I certainly didn't have to sail halfway around the world for that.

My parents simply smiled and put me on a boat to the United States.

---

[10] Reprinted by permission. *Footprints of a Pilgrim: The Life and Loves of Ruth Bell Graham* by Ruth Bell Graham © 2001, W. Publishing, Nashville, Tennessee. All rights reserved.

I was not happy.

It was early fall in 1940 when William Franklin Graham arrived on campus via the Wheaton College Student Trucking Service, run by Johnny Streater.

Billy Frank was a twenty-one-year-old North Carolinian, already an ordained Baptist minister, with clear blue eyes, standing six-foot-two....

On our first date we attended the school's presentation of the Messiah. "HALLELUJAH." I agonized over which of my two homemade dresses to wear.

After that first date, I knelt beside my bed and prayed, "God, if You let me serve You with that man, I'd consider it the greatest privilege of my life."

Billy Frank became the most popular subject in my journals, my poetry, and my letters. But our relationship went nowhere.

I began 1941 by flunking Greek and ancient history. Finally... February 7, he invited me to go to church to hear him preach.

I was surprised. He spoke with such authority...and, at the same time, humility. The star, seen and admired from afar, became a human, personal thing—within reach.

We drove back to campus in his 1937 green Plymouth. I watched his profile as he guided us through the Chicago traffic and marked the glint in his eyes where the streetlights flashed past. I had felt the firmness of his hand beneath my arm as he guided me through the crowd at the church. I was impressed by his unaffected thoughtfulness....

As he walked me to the door, he said, "There's something I'd like you to make a matter of prayer. I have been taking you out because I am more than interested in you and have been since the day Johnny Streater introduced us last fall. But I know you have been called to the mission field, and I'm not definite."

When Bill was young, he wanted to play professional baseball, and I wanted to go to Tibet. In truth, neither of us had any business doing either....

In September—"The Ring." It was purchased with every penny of the sixty-five dollar love offering Billy had received from Sharon Presbyterian Church.

God,
let me be all he ever dreamed
of loveliness and laughter.
Veil his eyes a bit
because
there are so many little flaws;
somehow, God,
please let him see
only the bride I long to be,
remembering ever after—
I was all he ever dreamed
of loveliness and laughter.

Those sentiments were rather youthful...and short-lived.

"I will not become a Baptist. I have always been and will always remain in the Presbyterian Church!"

"I'd like you to raise a family."

"I still think I should be a missionary."

"Listen, do you or do you not think the Lord brought us together?"

"Yes."

"Then I'll do the leading and you'll do the following."

I almost slapped the ring back into his hand—

Train our love...
Discipline it, too...
Deepen it
throughout the years,
age and mellow it
until, time that finds us
old without,
within,
will find us
lovers still.

I've been following ever since.

Father, You are the author of marriages made in Heaven. But it's not always easy to experience heaven on earth with the pressures of daily life. Help us to be of one heart and mind, to work together, to submit to one another, to quickly resolve conflicts, and to practice forgiveness. Fill our home with Your love and Your presence. Amen.

FRIEND'S FOR LIFE

Jackie's Story

By wisdom a house is built,
and through understanding it is established;
through knowledge its rooms are filled
with rare and beautiful treasures.

PROVERBS 24:3–4

"A counselor once told me that making a major life change is often the catalyst that forces people to deal with the emotional issues of their past. That was true in my case as the stress of a broken engagement ripped off the Band-Aid covering my wounded soul. I suddenly found my past come rushing to the present, forcing me to deal with issues I thought were solidly behind me," Jackie says, recalling the events of nearly twenty years ago.

Jackie's father walked out on her family when she was only ten. Her parents' turbulent marriage and a midlife crisis helped to push him over the edge and into the arms of another woman.

Although a professing Christian, he became involved in the deception we know today as the New Age movement and abandoned his Christian roots. Before this time, father and daughter had been very, very close, so the day he moved out, she says, "was the day the lights went out" for her.

"All of this transpired in the sixties, before divorce was commonplace," Jackie recounts. "My parents were the first to divorce in our circle of friends and family, so not only did I deal with heartbreak, there was shame because of the social stigma. The financial impact was devastating as well, as we went from an affluent lifestyle to my dad's total bankrupting of his once-profitable business. He began funneling huge sums of money into his new 'church,' until finally my mother began divorce proceedings, so we wouldn't lose our house."

This trauma affected Jackie's mom, brother, and her differently. Her mom turned to alcohol to help her cope with her pain and the uncertainties of having two young children to care for, during a time before many women had careers. Her brother acted out his anger and got into trouble at school, while Jackie's coping mechanism was to stuff all the negative emotions, "grab herself up by the bootstraps," and march on—a move she would later pay for.

Psychologists say that when young girls experience trauma, they usually deal with the issues later in life, while boys usually act out their pain closer to the time of the crisis. Jackie and her brother fit the profile to a T.

"To 'march on,' I felt I had to appear strong and together. I *never* allowed anyone to see the insecure, sad, and abandoned little girl that I was—terrified people would think less of me or feel sorry for me. Little did I realize that instead of protecting myself, these strong emotions became a ticking time bomb."

Always the model student and a leader in her peer group, Jackie demanded near perfection of herself. She *had* to make straight A's; she *had* to be part of the in crowd; she *had* to appear okay on the outside.

"I know now that this intense drive was my way of compensating for my feelings of inadequacy, the feeling that I was in some way defective because of the pain I carried inside," Jackie admits.

Tick, tick, tick...

But God was good. Not only was Jackie's mother miraculously delivered from alcoholism, Jackie, her mother, and her brother all had real-life encounters with God that turned their lives around and brought great healing.

After graduation from both high school and Bible school, Jackie began working for a Christian ministry where she could begin using her gifts and talents to help others. It was during this time that she met Jason—a tall, dark-haired, charismatic young man. Their mutual heart for God led to a strong attraction for one another, which quickly transformed into a whirlwind romance and engagement. She was quite literally swept off her feet. Life was good—for a while.

"When my mother met Jason for the first time, she felt great alarm inside. She *knew* he wasn't the right one for me, the same way she *knew* when my dad was entering dangerous territory with the cult. *And,* to complicate matters, my best friend felt the same way. Neither of them liked Jason and made no attempt to hide it. In my mind, my two closest allies had turned on me," Jackie remembers.

"For the next six months, I lived in utter turmoil. I could hardly eat or sleep. I was hopelessly in love with Jason and deeply hurt by my mother's and my friend's rejection of him. Yet, even in this confusion, I recognized that my mother was my spiritual covering. After all, she had been right about my dad's involvement with the cult. Was it possible that she was right this time too? Even though I was really hurt by the way she and my friend were handling the situation, I knew they loved me. I knew I had to at least consider what they were saying."

Tick, tick, tick...

As Jackie struggled with her churning emotions, the unbalanced area of her job became another factor contributing to the turmoil. Although she loved her job, it had become extremely stressful; and her need for approval had prevented her from setting boundaries to protect her from overwork. The increasing demands of both her position and the self-imposed perfectionism created mounting pressure that could no longer be ignored. Then, things began to sour with Jason.

"Slowly he began chipping away at my self-esteem, virtually trying to change everything about me—all the while letting me know how very selfish I was to resist his attempts to 'help' me," Jackie continues. "I had given this man my heart, yet it felt like he was jabbing me over and over again with the subtle yet consistent rejection."

Finally, the bomb exploded.

"The perceived lack of support from my mother and friend coupled with my stressful job and the pain of rejection from Jason blew the lid right off of the 'Pandora's box' of my wounded emotions. On top of that, I was no longer able to suppress the hurts and wounds of the past that I didn't even realize were there. It was a terrifying time, because I didn't understand what was happening to me. The always-in-control me was absolutely overcome by the tidal wave of emotions," she continues.

"A Christian counselor compared my life to trying to hold beach balls under water, the beach balls representing different trouble spots in my life. She explained that I could keep one or two down at the same time, but the more balls I added, the more they just kept popping up until I was completely unable to stop them."

Finally, after many months of what Jackie refers to as "sheer hell," it was like a fog cleared from her mind and she knew she had to end the relationship with Jason. It was as if God turned on the light and she finally saw Jason for the wolf in sheep's clothing that he was. But the damage had been done. Jackie felt like the man in the Good Samaritan story who was left bleeding to death on the side of the road—totally abandoned. Jason was gone, and her relationships with her mother and best friend had been mortally wounded. She was a mess.

"While I had felt worthless before, now I *knew* I was worthless," Jackie recalls. "My road to recovery was a slow one, but the healing began at church."

During the first Sunday service after Jason was out of her life, in her mind's eye she saw herself bowed to the floor in front of Jesus during the worship time, totally broken, so disappointed that her "fairy-tale" romance had turned out to be a nightmare. As she was worshiping at the feet of Jesus, her tears soaking her clothes, she saw Him reach out His hand to her and gently say, *Stand up. You don't belong there on the floor. You belong up here with Me.*

"I felt so loved—cherished, treasured. I caught a glimpse of how much He valued me, and I felt safe," Jackie says. "I can't overstate the impact this encounter had on me. But anytime God speaks to you, it leaves an indelible mark. It provided the breakthrough that I needed to get back on track."

It would take several years for Jackie to fully recover from the complex issues she was dealing with, but healing did come—spiritually, physically, and emotionally. God divinely brought people, books, information, and a multitude of other things into her life to help her rebuild the foundations of her life.

It was during this season of rebuilding that she met David.

"I knew better than to get involved in a rebound relationship, especially being as vulnerable as I was. Yet here was this amazing, godly man who had entered my life. I was terrified of making another wrong decision in getting involved with anyone, but David just wanted to be my friend. Somehow God gave him the grace to see past the basket case I had become down to the real me on the inside struggling to emerge.

"One valuable lesson I gained from my relationship with Jason was that you have nothing to lose by taking a relationship slowly, while you have everything to lose by going too fast. Going fast almost caused me to make the biggest mistake of my life. Thankfully, David was patient. We took our relationship very slowly, taking great pains to be completely open and honest with one another. No game-playing, no deception. We were both able to share out hurts from the past and receive genuine comfort and acceptance from one another. David was a gentle man, deeply committed to God, and I knew he would be a friend for life, and he felt the same about me.

"Because we wanted to guard this precious friendship, we did not become physically involved in any way. Once that line is crossed, even by holding hands or a simple kiss, a relationship takes on an entirely different meaning—and I knew from experience that physical involvement can cloud one's thinking and hinder the ability to hear God's voice. That's probably not for everyone, but we knew it was right for us," Jackie shares openly.

Month after month David and Jackie discussed their different backgrounds, the family dynamics they grew up with, their opposite personality types, their methods of communication, how they felt about money and children, the vision each had of the future. No stone was left unturned as they worked through difficult issues that many people wait till after they are married to deal with—things that can become so-called "irreconcilable differences" that often lead to the divorce court. They didn't want to wind up in that position, preferring instead to find their place of agreement before they found themselves in the heat of an argument.

You've probably guessed by now. David and Jackie did marry. (Incidentally, her best friend was thrilled, and her mom loved David and still does.) Because they had laid the groundwork long before the wedding, they did not have the huge adjustment period that is common during the first year of marriage. In fact, Jackie says it was more like a yearlong honeymoon. She says that their entire relationship has been a bit of heaven on earth.

"David and I both know that we can't take credit for what we have, other than we have involved God in our relationship every step of the way," Jackie concludes as we talk. "Sure, we've had challenges—life happens—but the deep friendship that we built during our season of dating laid a strong and solid foundation that has made it much easier for us to work through things as they've come up. We are still each other's very best friend.

"The bottom line? A happy marriage is possible; it is God's plan. And no matter what you walk through in life, nothing is too difficult for God to fix and heal. My life is proof of that, and I'm eternally grateful."

Dear God, You are the only One who knows the depth of my pain, for You have been with me every step of the way. You are the healer and restorer, and I give You permission to do Your deep work in me. Should You bring someone into my life to marry, may we conduct ourselves in such a way during our courtship that we will have no regrets in the future. Help us to build a strong foundation on which to build our lives. Amen.

The Richest Man in the World

John's Story

The man who finds a wife finds a good thing;
she is a blessing to him from the Lord.

PROVERBS 18:22 TLB

"Hey, Teresa! When are we going out?" the athletic senior quipped, as he passed the pretty blond student in the school office.

The question was not an actual request, nor did John expect a response. Yet somehow it had become a game, a challenge. It first started in a conversation with the guys.

"Teresa and I had only talked a couple of times at school, but she had always been kind toward me," John recalls. "So when I heard some of my buddies referring to her in the form of a conquest, I felt compelled to defend her."

"Ain't nobody gettin' no action with her," one stated.

I really hated that kind of talk, especially since Teresa was a Christian. I wanted to change the subject. "Obviously none of you hound dogs is the right person," I replied.

"So, you think you could get her to kiss *you* on the first date?" they challenged.

Something about that conversation lodged in John's mind, creating an unconscious shift in his previously casual relationship with Teresa.

As a senior in high school, John had already excelled in many areas. He was president of the French club, the history club, and the honor society. He also excelled with girls and had developed a reputation as a ladies' man, but in reality he felt very alone.

"My home life was less than perfect," John recalls. "I had seven brothers and sisters as my family became mixed in Brady-Bunch fashion. Only ours was not always a happy family."

What John longed for was a stable, loving relationship.

Prior to that conversation with the guys, John had never seriously considered dating Teresa. She was one of the "good" girls; and, well, that just wasn't his type. Still, he jokingly commented about a date each time he saw her.

His position as president of the honor society required frequent interaction with the school counselor. As a senior, Teresa sometimes worked in the office, so their paths crossed frequently.

Entering the counselor's office one afternoon in a thinly veiled guise to skip English class, John passed Teresa. As if on cue, he rattled off the now familiar line, "Hey, when are we going out?" Smiling to himself, he walked in to see the counselor.

A couple of minutes later, as Teresa walked past the office, she slowly retraced her steps. Popping her head in, she actually responded to John's question for the first time.

"Well, whenever you ask," she smiled before walking on again.

"I was dumbfounded," John said. "The situation had turned serious in an instant. What had been my ongoing joke had suddenly turned into a joke on me. And while I had not always done the right thing in my relationships with girls, I had a sense of honor when it came to Teresa and wanted to treat her right."

Excusing himself from the counselor, John walked out to find Teresa, fully intending to set the record straight and apologize. The next thing he heard coming out of his mouth shocked Teresa as well as him. "Hey, Teresa. I'm asking," he stated.

There was a long pause, but as John's mind raced with the thought of what he had just said, he realized he didn't want to take the words back. Two weeks later, they had their first official date.

"Although I wasn't of legal age, I ordered a drink, hoping to impress her; but the things that impressed other girls didn't impress Teresa," John shares about that evening.

"I would prefer that you not drink," she commented calmly after we left the restaurant. There was something so compelling about the way she had made her feelings known, that I never took another drink again," John confides.

"Much to my surprise, I did get a kiss on our first date. My mind immediately recalled the conversation with the guys, "You think you're the right guy?" That kiss hooked me into staying with the relationship as I contemplated for the first time the possibility that this girl just might be the one for me. The more I considered the relationship, I was finally able to admit to myself that I was slowly falling in love with her."

Although John's heart toward Teresa was changing, his attitude toward God was not, even though their dates typically centered around prayer meetings and revival services. John went with Teresa only because he wanted to be with her. She continued dating him only because she felt he would change. But there was no indication that the services they attended were having any impact whatsoever on his life.

"At one such service, I remembered very little except to admire the gift of delivery from the fiery evangelist. Afterwards as we made our way out of the church, I shook his hand and expressed my appreciation for his oratory skill, even though I hadn't understood his message. 'That was a great speech,' I complimented.

"The preacher pulled back his hand as if I had slapped his face," John laughs in remembrance. "'Sir, you need to pray for yourself,' he directed."

Still in spiritual darkness, John couldn't understand what had offended the evangelist. But although it couldn't be seen on the surface, Teresa's prayers and the words of the preachers were having an effect on him.

From that time on, the services John and Teresa attended became increasingly uncomfortable for John. No longer could he sit complacently in the back. Now each time he entered a church, the words of the evangelist came flooding back into his mind, *Sir, you need to pray for yourself.*

"I realized I didn't even know how to pray for myself and whispered aloud, 'God, if You're real, show me.'"

And He did.

John found over the next few weeks that his prayer in those services had changed. It was no longer, "God, if You're real, show me," but now became, "God, I know You're real. What do I need to do?"

Finally, at the close of yet another service, John listened as the worship leader kept singing the old song, "Just as I Am." About the eighth time of singing the chorus, he finally slammed the hymnal shut in surrender. "Lord, save me," he whispered.

"I knew even before I left my seat to walk forward that I had been changed. I was different...and I knew I was called to preach. *And* about three weeks later, I knew I was to marry Teresa. But I didn't dare tell her that—not yet."

At the end of the summer, Teresa left for college in another state, while John remained in North Carolina to attend the community college. They knew the period of separation would be difficult, but it became increasingly challenging when Teresa met a young man on her school campus. Although unwilling to admit it, Teresa was strongly attracted to her classmate's spiritual depth, something John didn't yet possess. Over the next several weeks, it became increasingly clear to John via their letters and phone conversations that the girl he loved was slipping away.

But what Teresa couldn't see was that John was maturing fast.

"In just the few weeks I had been a believer, I had already read a considerable portion of the Old and New Testaments. And although new in my commitment to Christ, I was already teaching a Sunday school class, testifying and giving mini-sermons, and became involved with the choir. I was so hungry for God that my faith and knowledge of Him were growing by leaps and bounds," John states.

As the school year progressed, Teresa became increasingly more confused about the two men in her life. As the emotional turmoil intensified, she made the decision to leave school for a week to return home ostensibly to be with her family. In reality, she had gone home to make up her mind. Unfortunately, it seemed from the beginning of her visit that her decision had already been made.

"After her arrival, we arranged to meet at the Wednesday night church service. Her change in attitude toward me was immediately apparent as she greeted me briefly only to walk away to sit with her parents for the service," John shares. "My heart felt constricted as I debated whether or not to walk out and away from the painful distance that separated us. But I couldn't. I loved Teresa. I made the decision to stay, no matter the outcome.

"After the service Teresa almost reluctantly agreed to stay behind and talk. As the church emptied, we eventually decided to take a drive to continue our conversation. Although alone, there was no physical contact between us. We were just two friends getting reacquainted. I could only hope that Teresa could see the growth that had taken place in my life since she left.

"Finally, that weekend over dinner, I pressed Teresa for a decision. 'Teresa, I need to know if I am just a friend or if there is something more between us.'

"Over the previous several days, Teresa was able to see for herself the metamorphosis that had taken place in my life. She didn't hesitate in giving her answer—the one I had hoped for."

John and Teresa became engaged later that year, setting a wedding date for the summer before their senior year of college, two years away. The next year John transferred schools to join Teresa, and their relationship continued to deepen.

"Those were the happiest times I had ever had. I loved her more than anyone I had ever loved in my life. She seemed to be everything I needed—loving, caring, compassionate, and most of all, forgiving of my past," John continues his story.

After completing their junior year, Teresa returned home immediately to finalize plans for their July wedding. John stayed behind to continue working and, in his spare time, he kept studying the Bible. Everything seemed to be going perfectly.

After returning to North Carolina, Teresa got a job interning as a social worker—her major. The work was not strenuous, but Teresa seemed to have difficulty keeping up with the physical demands of the position. Her energy level decreased to the point that she finally went to the doctor. While the doctor confirmed the low energy level, he had no explanation for the cause and ordered an array of tests.

Two weeks later, John got a call from Teresa's mother. Emotion choked her voice as she finally communicated the message, "John, the doctor's report came back on Teresa. She has just two years to live."

Teresa had been diagnosed with cardio pulmonary hyper-tension, a disease that creates a higher than normal pressure in the lungs, ultimately causing the heart to enlarge on one side and become deformed. Teresa was growing weaker and weaker.

"The pain from her mother's words pierced me like a sword. In my mind, Teresa was irreplaceable. She was the missing puzzle piece in my life, and for the first time I felt whole and valuable. I couldn't believe the diagnosis," John explains.

"Later, Teresa's mom told me that she and her husband had met with my parents and that they all felt that it would be the right thing to call off the wedding. Logically I could see their point," John admits. "But this wasn't about logic. It was a matter of the heart. I told her that I wanted to talk to Teresa about it, that it needed to be her decision.

"Once Teresa came to the phone, I told her, 'Your parents think we shouldn't get married. I'm willing to call it off, if it is what you want.' Then, after a short pause, I asked, 'What do you think?'

"I prayed silently as Teresa pondered the question.

"'It would break my heart,' she said quietly.

"It would have broken mine too," John confesses.

John and Teresa married in a simple ceremony two weeks later. By that time, Teresa had grown so weak physically that John had to help her stand as they exchanged their vows, but what she lacked in energy she made up for with the joy in their marriage.

Within days of their return to Tulsa, in preparation for their final year at the university, John realized that Teresa would be unable to continue. Her condition had deteriorated so rapidly that he couldn't take care of her by himself, so he made plans to return to their family and friends back home.

In preparation for the trip, John checked Teresa into the hospital. She had been unable to eat and needed nutrients through IVs to strengthen her frail body. But Teresa never left the hospital. They had been married only fifty days.

"Even in the pain of Teresa's death, my parents and I experienced new life," John explains. "Little did I know, my parents had been watching me during the trying days immediately after Teresa's death. The witness of the strength that was not my own, that carried me through the grief of my loss, conveyed more than words ever could have. They gave their lives to Christ within a week of each other."

Not long after, at only twenty-one years of age, John returned to Oklahoma to restart a life that had no one in it anymore. Months passed before he could even contemplate the mere thought of ever allowing another woman into his life. But as his heart began to heal, God began to prepare him for a new season.

Around this time, John and his roommate went out for dinner one night. Their waitress was a pretty blonde Bible-school student with a bubbly personality. Something about this stranger sparked John's interest. As they prepared to depart, he left her a note on the table, "It's nice to meet you. I'd like to get to know you better."

Two weeks later, he returned to the restaurant and asked her out. Although they dated for the next couple of months, by then it seemed obvious, at least to John, that their lives were heading in different directions. Lori was just eighteen at the time and after the road John had walked, she seemed incredibly young to him. He knew it was time to go their separate ways before it became too painful.

"In all honesty, Lori faced an insurmountable barrier with the memory of my former wife, whom I had elevated to the level of sainthood," John admits. "No one would have been able to live up to the standard I had unconsciously set."

The bottom line was, John wasn't ready for a new relationship yet. God still had some work to do in him before he could really let go of his past. And without letting go of the past, he couldn't fully embrace the future God had for him.

After their breakup, Lori returned to her family in Arizona; and John resumed the task of rebuilding his life—comfortable, he thought, with his decision. That is until he ran into her later that summer at a swimming pool. The moment he saw her, he realized how much he had missed her. Although Lori had returned to Tulsa for only a brief visit, they began dating again. It wasn't long before John recognized the awakening of deeper feelings.

Never one to waste time on futile efforts, John suddenly needed to know if God's plan was for him to marry again. Although his mind was having to catch up to his spirit, deep inside, he knew marriage was His will.

Now John just needed to know if Lori was the woman God had chosen for him. "On a whim I invited Lori to go with me to Dallas where my parents had moved. Although I was fairly certain that she was the one for me, I needed to know for sure. The entire trip, I listened intently for God's voice and scrutinized Lori's actions as well as my feelings. In a way this was unfair to Lori, but I knew the stakes were too high for either of us to make a mistake. Unless this was God's will, the relationship would be doomed to failure."

As the day wore on, John began to waver in his thinking as various emotions washed over him. Later that night after Lori had gone to bed in the guest room, he sat in the kitchen with his mom.

"She's not Teresa," he began.

John's mother provided a listening ear as John talked through the turmoil in his heart. Finally, he headed to bed, having convinced himself that there was no future in the relationship.

But during the night John had three separate dreams that were interrelated. At the beginning, a single apple tree grew in the middle of a luscious green field. It was a mature tree, full of beautiful white blossoms that swayed in the gentle breeze. A warm feeling came over him as he stared at the tree.

In the second dream, the tree was budding with small green fruit all over its branches. Finally, close to morning time, he had a third dream, only this time the tree was covered with fruit that was mature and ripe. The branches were so heavy laden that they almost touched the ground.

"After each dream I heard the words, *Would you chop down this tree?*

"Never, Lord," I replied with conviction. "Your Word says that every tree is known by its fruit. This tree has good fruit."

Instantly John awoke with the understanding that the "tree" represented Lori.

"God knew that I had begun to waver from the peace He had put in my heart. He knew I had been on the verge of making the biggest mistake of my life, and in His mercy, He intervened in a profound way. I got up immediately and knocked on the door to Lori's room, now certain of the next step in God's plan for my life.

"Will you marry me?" I asked.

"Thankfully, she accepted, and I've never looked back."

Today a wooden apple sits on John's dresser as a reminder of that prophetic dream that altered the course of their lives. Lori and John have been married twenty–three years now; they have eight children and work together full time in children's ministry.

"Lori makes me better than I could have even been by myself," says John. "People that observe us say that we are like two halves of a circle, each completing the other.

"Yes, Teresa was, at that time, a love greater than anything I had ever experienced, and I will forever honor her memory. But as is always the case with God, He took a tragedy and turned it into the biggest miracle of my life when He gave Lori to me. She is exactly what I need, handpicked by God; and the love we share is deeper than I even knew was possible. Because of her and our precious children, I am the richest man in the world."

Heavenly Father, just as only You can make a flower grow in the middle of the desert, only You can provide miracles for us in the midst of painful and barren times in our lives. Never are we without hope. There are always brighter days ahead in You. Amen.

JOHN AND LORI BANNER are children's pastors at Victory Christian Center in Tulsa, Oklahoma. Together, they have dedicated their lives to the purpose of reaching children for Jesus Christ. Their family has ministered together in churches, camps, and on the mission field for over fifteen years. "I am always mindful of the years I wasted before I began living for Christ," John shares. "We want to do all we can to rescue this generation of kids before they need to be rescued."

Who Says You Can't Mix Business with Pleasure?

Dave and Karen's Story

A wife of noble character who can find?
She is worth far more than rubies.
Her husband has full confidence in her
and lacks nothing of value.

Proverbs 31:10–11

"On our very first date, Dave must have asked me one hundred and twenty questions!" Karen exclaims with a laugh.

Both in their late twenties at the time, Dave approached dating the same way he approached every other aspect of his life, in a very pragmatic, no-nonsense manner. At least in his reasoning, what was the sense in dating a girl who had absolutely no possibility of being marriage material? No, they were both too old to play the dating game just for kicks, so

Dave quizzed Karen throughout the evening, turning the event into a marathon question–and–answer session.

"Toward the end of the evening as he was taking me home, he asked me how many kids I wanted someday." That was when things got really interesting, Karen remembers. "When I told him five, he exclaimed, 'Five kids?!'"

"I had in my mind that one day I would marry, have two point five kids and a nice, comfortable home," Dave shares. "So my response was, 'Five kids? No way!'"

In spite of this minor discrepancy, Dave continued to ask Karen out. Within five months, he was certain that she was the one for him and began making plans for a very romantic proposal.

"As a businessman I wanted plenty of time not only to plan the details of the proposal, but also to make sure of the answer I was going to receive," Dave laughs. "Who wants to propose, only to be turned down?" So, after much deliberation, Dave established his plan.

"I wanted to propose to Karen on Valentine's Day," Dave explains. "Not just on the day, but at the very *beginning* of the day, at the stroke of midnight," he shares, as the plot thickens.

Never one to do things halfheartedly, Dave made plans that incorporated an all–day trip to Dallas, a romantic meal over–looking the skyline as the sun set, and finally a very special proposal upon returning home.

"Oh, and don't forget the small business deal in the middle of the trip so that it could be tax deductible!" Karen reminds him with a grin.

Dave laughs as he shares with me the events of that day.

"I told Karen that I wanted her to go to the airport with me to pick up a friend. She readily agreed. But as we sat at the terminal and the plane unloaded, my 'friend' never got off the plane."

"I wonder where he is?" Karen asked.

"Maybe we can go aboard the plane and look," Dave responded, knowing full well there was no friend to be found.

As they approached the gate, they were stopped by a flight attendant. "I'm sorry, sir. You can't go on board without a ticket."

"We don't have a ticket," Karen responded, only to be interrupted by Dave.

"You mean these tickets?" Dave offered the stewardess.

"Karen was so surprised and got really excited as we boarded the plane," Dave shares. "We were off to a good start."

After landing, Dave and Karen were off to the upscale Prestonwood shopping area, where they had a nice lunch and window-shopped. Then Dave made that quick stop to talk with one of his clients.

"It took about two hours!" Karen remembers, good-naturedly. "And I even typed some of the business forms for the transaction."

"That way your part of the trip could be deducted as well," Dave banters back, a smile in his voice.

"I had timed the day so that we could arrive at the restaurant for our evening meal while it was still daylight, yet also be able to watch the sun set and enjoy the glimmering lights at nightfall," Dave continues. "I had made our reservations at this restaurant months in advance. It was the well-known Antares Restaurant at Reunion Tower. The very top floor is a glass-enclosed revolving restaurant that looks out over the expansive Dallas skyline."

"I started getting nervous because I thought he was going to propose right then," Karen says.

But the couple finished their meal and walked back to their rental car to return to the airport and their flight back home.

"It had been a perfect day," Dave states. "Even on the way to the airport, the radio station played one of my favorite songs at the time by the Sweet Comfort Band, 'Love You with My Life.' The song held special meaning for us as I had often sung it to Karen during our dates. And another one of our favorite songs had played just before that."

It was almost as if God had arranged a special serenade for the couple on their very special day.

As the plane landed, Dave realized they still had time to kill before reaching the time and place he had planned for the proposal. Taking his time, he took Karen on an extended tour of the city, revisiting sites that had been memorable throughout their dating relationship. The place where they had their first date; the park where they first kissed; until finally, it was just fifteen minutes to midnight as Dave made his way to the beautiful prayer garden of their alma mater.

As they sat on one of the benches, Dave pulled out a card he had written for Karen with sweet sentiments of his love. As she finished reading, he announced, "Karen, it is now midnight—Valentine's Day—and I have a very important question to ask you."

Getting down on bended knee, he finally brought the evening to its intended climax, "Will you marry me?"

"Karen just started to cry," Dave states. "I didn't know what that meant and was slightly apprehensive that she might be upset over the proposal and wasn't going to accept. It seemed like an hour and a half before she found her voice and finally answered. In reality it was probably only thirty seconds, but her silence seemed endless."

Smiling through her tears, Karen agreed as they sealed their engagement with a hug and a romantic kiss.

As with many couples, Dave and Karen have had to learn to blend their very different personalities into a harmonious union. For example, Karen vividly remembers the first day of their honeymoon. Sitting on their hotel balcony overlooking the ocean in Hawaii, she wanted nothing more than to bask in the moment, a moment that was shattered as Dave walked up with two pencils and notepads. Laying one set on the table beside Karen, he turned and with all seriousness said, "Why don't we write down our goals for the next year, five years, and then ten years?"

Always the businessman, Dave had an agenda for their future, but it is an agenda that has worked well for them.

"In all fairness, he is quite the romantic even after all these years of marriage," Karen is quick to insert.

And remember that small discrepancy over the number of kids? Well, that has been easily resolved since Dave and Karen have both received just what they wanted. Karen has her five and Dave has his two as their six boys and one girl round out this very happy family.

Dear God, You are such a romantic! Thank You for creating so many places of beauty where we can share our love and be creative in our expression of it. Courtship is such a special time in a couple's life as well as the honeymoon and beyond. Marriage, romance, children, and happy families are all Your idea, and I bless You for it. Amen.

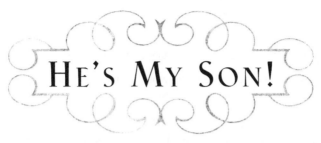

He's My Son!

Love does not delight in evil but rejoices with the truth.

1 Corinthians 13:6

The audience grew quiet as the two women entered the courtroom, their apparel revealing their unsavory occupation. Most looked away in disgust, while others looked on with growing curiosity until one of the women spoke to the king.

"My lord, this woman and I live in the same house. I had a baby while she was there with me. The third day after my child was born, this woman also had a baby. We were alone; there was no one in the house but the two of us. During the night, this woman's son died because she lay on him. So she got up in the middle of the night and took my son from my side while I, your servant, was asleep. She put him by her breast and put her dead son by my breast. The next morning, I got up to nurse my son—and he was dead! But when I looked at him closely in the morning light, I saw that it wasn't the son I had borne."

"No!" screamed the woman beside her, oblivious to the crowd. The living one is my son. The dead one is yours.

"He isn't," the other woman hollered in response. "You think I can't recognize my own son? He's mine!"

The heated argument escalated as the wise king looked on.

"Enough!" he silenced the women by the authority in his voice. "I'll settle the matter fairly.

"Bring me a sword," he instructed. Upon his command a sharp blade was handed to the king as he rose before the two women. "Now bring me the child."

The crowd gasped as the small infant was brought before the king.

Looking directly at the women, he spoke, "This is my verdict. Cut the living child in two and give half to one and half to the other," the king instructed, handing the sword over to his guard.

It was at that moment that true love spoke up.

"Please, my lord, give her the baby! Don't kill him!" cried one.

The woman next to her sneered as she said, "Neither I nor you shall have him. Cut him in two!"

Immediately King Solomon raised his hand to the guard to stop the gruesome sacrifice. "Give the baby to the first woman. Do not kill him; she is his mother."[11]

LIFE LESSONS

1. True love—whether it is romantic love, sacrificial love, enduring love—all comes from God, for He is love.

[11] Story based upon 1 Kings 3:16–21, 26–27.

2. True love looks out not for its own interests, but for the interests of others. One can always recognize true love when willing to look with a wise heart.
3. There are many times that love is professed, but words and actions are greater indicators than words alone.

SECTION
6

Second Chances

If you have made mistakes, even serious mistakes,
there is always another chance for you.
And supposing you have tried and failed again
and again, you may have a fresh start any moment
you choose, for this thing that we call "failure"
is not the falling down, but the staying down.

MARY PICKFORD

The God of Second Chances

Thomas and Juanita Bynum Weeks[12]

[Love] always protects, always trusts, always hopes, always perseveres. Love never fails.

1 Corinthians 13:7–8

Trinity Broadcasting Network televised the wedding celebration of Bishop Thomas Weeks and Rev. Juanita Bynum to millions of viewers last year. It was a widely celebrated union, the second marriage for both.

Have you ever wondered if there will be a second chance for you? Thankfully, we serve a God who specializes in second

---

[12] Reprinted with permission. Thomas Weeks III, *Teach Me How to Love You* (Denver: CO, Legacy Publishers International © 2003) pp. 9, 17–18, 63.

chances. This is not to say that He approves of divorce. In fact, the Bible says He hates it because of the damage it does to the hearts and lives of those left in its wake. But if you have already walked through the pain of a broken relationship and now find yourself alone, rest assured, God is not finished with you yet.

The Bible is full of examples of second chances. Some of the more prominent individuals are King David (2 Sam. 11 and 12), Jehoshaphat (2 Chron. 20), and the apostle Paul (Acts 9:4–9). Repeatedly throughout the Old and New Testaments, we read of men and women from all walks of life who failed in one area or another. Yet once they submitted their hearts to God and repented of their sin, God restored. The following is one such story.

"My wife has been through many disappointments with men," shares author and minister, Thomas Wesley Weeks III. "On two different occasions she was abandoned by a fiancé who immediately turned around and married another woman. There were other times she suffered emotional and physical abuse and was used to satisfy a man's personal and financial needs.

"She loved the Lord, but she made a bad relationship choice that eventually brought her to the point of trying to take her own life. That's when God spoke to her. He told her to fulfill her marriage vows. She remained faithful to her commitment until the day her husband said, 'It's time for me to go.' He gave her the keys and never came back.

"Thinking back several years to my own experience, I had gone from being married and enjoying a successful life to being alone with barely enough to survive. For two years, I went through a painful process in which God tested my commitment to His will. I lost everything, even friends in the ministry. People stopped inviting me to preach and every door seemed to be slamming in my face. That's when I learned to give all my praises to God. That's when God birthed a new vision in me," Weeks finishes.

"Both Wesley and I have learned hard lessons about love in the past," Juanita picks up the conversation. "So we don't take our love for granted. We work at it. And so should you, if you want your marriage to survive and grow. I spent almost twenty years waiting for God to bring my husband because I had learned that unwise decisions could lead to disaster and heartbreak."

After years of singleness and a process of healing from past hurts, Weeks and Bynum met and began dating. But as with any relationship, there were challenges that had to be worked out or they would have had to abandon the relationship.

Weeks shares of one defining instance in that process: "One Saturday afternoon (following a wonderful Friday evening date at the theater), Juanita and I experienced our first conversational difficulty (better known to others as an argument). We both had such different views of the situation that we couldn't bring it to terms. Finally, after much 'heated fellowship,' we decided to meet at Starbuck's and discuss a way to solve the issue.

"I was pretty tense and nervous while waiting for her to arrive, yet, I was confident that God had called me to be her husband. And I understood that I would need to make the sacrifice at this meeting, not her. However, when Juanita stepped out of her car, she took ten steps toward me and opened her arms. I walked to her and we embraced. At that moment, I knew even more surely that there was a covenant between us that needed to be kept and nurtured.

"We went into Starbuck's, ordered two of our favorite drinks, and began to dialogue about what we felt was wrong at that point in our relationship. Interestingly, the sensitive things she shared only confirmed what had already been in my spirit about how I truly needed to love her.

"As tears began to run down her cheeks, I moved in close, grabbed her hands, and placed them on my chest as if to say, 'Feel me; I know where you're at.' Then I looked deep in her eyes and said, 'Teach me how to love you.'"

From that conversation, both Weeks and Bynum were able to reach deeper into their hearts, past their own needs and hurts, to build a strong foundation that this time would last.

"True love is under attack," Juanita continues. "Christian marriages are failing right and left because too many believers are trying to love according to the world's concepts. We're too timid about what really works and what really matters when it comes to having a godly relationship.

"I'm so blessed that God has given me a man of the Word. And every day, I try to please and support my husband, bringing out the best God has already deposited in him. This is our commitment. This is a true marriage. This is the kind of marriage that will overcome the enemy every time."

Heavenly Father, I'm so thankful that You are a God of second chances. Thank You for Your willingness to forgive and cleanse me of my shortcomings and failures. Help me to move past them by Your grace and to learn from them so I won't make the same mistakes in the future. Help me to live a life that honors You. Amen.

Can You Help Me Raise My Son?

Susi's Story

Do not dwell on the past.
See, I am doing a new thing!
Now it springs up; do you not perceive it?
I am making a way in the desert
and streams in the wasteland.

Isaiah 43:18–19

Mike and Lisa Taylor had been married approximately two years when God brought Susi into their lives. So far, without children of their own, they knew they were to help her raise her three young daughters. What they didn't know was that Susi was going to raise their son.

Recently widowed, Susi was left with three girls ranging in ages five to thirteen. Her husband, Boyce, had been killed in a freak accident during a business trip—an accident about which she had first been told that her husband was expected to live.

Gary, who accompanied Boyce on the trip, called from the hospital: "Susi, it's a miracle. He doesn't even have any broken bones. I'll call you back when we know more." It was indeed a miracle.

Boyce and Gary had been returning from Texarkana while pulling their mobile office trailer behind their jeep. Suddenly, Gary lost control of the vehicle. The trailer began to spin out of control, flipping the jeep and trailer twice. On the first turn, Boyce flew out the window. On the second, the trailer rolled over him. Miraculously not a single bone was broken.

But Boyce *didn't* make it. As doctors inflated a collapsed lung, they inadvertently released the pressure that had stopped the flow of blood from his severed main artery. Before doctors could figure out what had happened, Boyce was gone.

"Lord, what am I going to do?" Susi cried out to God after she received the news. In her heart, she heard a distinct reply, *Susi, the plan has never changed.*

As Susi took a deep breath, she remembered an unusual occurrence that she now recognized as God's preparation for the very news she had just received. She had been visited by an angel.

Susi isn't someone who just attends church on Sundays and calls herself a Christian. Hers is a personal relationship with God. Talking with Him throughout the day is as natural and real as talking with her children. And it's not a one-sided conversation as God speaks to her through Scripture or impresses something upon her heart. But an angelic visitation? She had heard others speak of them, but had never had such an experience herself until one fall evening in September 1991. During that time, the angel spoke a word from the Lord: *In four months, you will begin the next chapter of your life.*

"I didn't have any idea what that meant until a few weeks later a close friend asked me to reenter the work force. Since the birth of my children, I had quit working as a hair and makeup artist for movies and television events. The hours were long and Boyce and I had gone into full-time ministry. I had closed my business in order to give my young children the time they needed."

Then, out of the blue, the opportunity to restart her career was presented through a good friend who just happened to have a thriving business in the same uncommon vocation. With her children now older, the timing seemed right, so Susi agreed, taking various assignments. Now with the unexpected death of her husband, exactly four months to the day of that angelic visitation, Susi was faced with the sole financial responsibility for her family. At least, through her work, they would have some income.

"It was actually through that job that I met Lisa Taylor and eventually her husband, Mike," Susi explains. "Shortly after I returned to work, I assisted with the hair and makeup for one of Carman's contemporary Christian music videos. Lisa worked for Carman and we became good friends."

Although the Taylors had only known Susi a couple of months when Boyce died, they immediately stepped in to help.

"Mike and Lisa were such a blessing," Susi recalls. "They would take the kids to the doctor for me or stay with them until my baby-sitter would show up when I had to work. Mike would take them to basketball games and literally stepped into the role of the father they no longer had."

The two families became so close that Lisa and Mike began asking Susi and her kids to join them for holidays with Lisa's family. Together they helped Susi raise her young family. And then they found out that Lisa was pregnant!

"Mike and Lisa had already been married about six years, so we were all rejoicing at the news," Susi shares. "But from the beginning, there were complications."

Over the eight-month pregnancy, Susi took Lisa to the doctor several times; twice for heart palpitations for which she was sent to a heart specialist.

"Just sitting in the sun would cause her to get extremely flushed, and she never seemed to feel good during the pregnancy," Susi continues.

Finally, as Lisa's condition worsened, the doctors made the decision to perform a C-section, both for the protection of the baby and to provide more medical assistance to Lisa. On Thanksgiving Day 1994, Cole was born, a healthy little boy in spite of his early arrival. But Lisa wasn't faring as well.

"Are we out of the woods yet?" Lisa asked their mutual friend, Dr. John, who had come by the hospital to visit.

"Not by a long shot," Dr. John informed Mike later. Lisa's blood platelets were extremely low and she was very weak. Lisa was hooked up to life support and it became a one-day-at-a-time vigil. Just six days after Cole's birth, the doctors informed Mike that Lisa was gone.

"Mike didn't know what to do," Susi shares.

Lisa's mom came to help with the baby for a while, but eventually she had to return home and Mike had to return to his job as a traveling sales representative for a sporting goods firm. There was no way he could take care of the baby by himself. That's when he decided to find a nanny.

"It was hysterical," Susi recalls. "Mike would sit facing the interviewee, and Dr. John and I would be standing behind them. Whenever we felt one didn't qualify, we would slide a finger across our throats, signaling the person's cut from the interview. None of the ladies ever realized what we were doing, but it worked quite effectively," Susi laughs.

After interviewing numerous candidates, Mike became discouraged. He didn't trust leaving his newborn son with a single one of the applicants. But something had to be done.

"Susi, we have a responsibility to help Mike raise his son," Dr. John said to her, shortly after the failed interview attempts.

"What he really meant wasn't 'we' but 'me,'" Susi laughs.

Susi had been praying regarding the situation, so she wasn't taken by surprise when Mike approached her about helping him to raise Cole.

Susi agreed.

"Cole immediately moved in with the girls and me," says Susi. "Mike had to leave on another business trip, so the agreement was made and he was off.

"The girls were ecstatic. They loved little Cole and treated him like a little brother. When Mike was in town, he would help watch the kids. When I was off work and he was gone, I would watch the kids. It may sound like a strange arrangement to some, but it worked for us," Susi explains.

About six months later during one of Mike's visits, he surprised Susi with another question. "Do you think there is any way we could ever become romantic with each other?"

"It may seem obvious, but I had never thought of Mike in that way," Susi now explains.

But the more she considered their close friendship, his love for her daughters, and her love for Cole, the relationship made more and more sense. Once Susi opened her heart to the thought, much to her surprise, their once pragmatic relationship quickly blossomed into love. Three months later, Mike and Susi made the arrangement official.

"Not only did our parents attend the wedding," Susi states, "but so did my first mother-in-law and Lisa's parents.

Although it happened quickly, I think it was evident to everyone that God had His hand on our relationship.

"I believe that God is moving a miracle toward us every single day," Susi finishes her story. "He isn't mad or angry with us. He isn't distant from us. Instead, He desires to walk with us and bless us. God doesn't cause the difficult events in our life, but He certainly walks with us as we go through them."

Heavenly Father, You aren't the author of tragedy, but You are the God who sees ahead and makes provision for us. Thank You for never leaving me without support or provision. You are truly the God who is more than enough for me. Amen.

From Sonic to a Supernatural Marriage

Quita's Story

Those who sow in tears will reap with songs of joy.

Psalm 126:5

At twenty-six, Quita had been approved to move into a small duplex in government housing. All she had was a bed, a couch and chair, her piano, her two boys, and a peace from God that filled her heart in spite of her present conditions.

"It was a place to start over," remembers Quita. "In my mind it seemed like an unusual place for restoration, but God assured me that it was where He wanted us for the time being."

Just a year before, she had been a happily married pastor's wife with a loving family. But her fairy-tale bubble popped almost overnight.

Quita married on her nineteenth birthday. Approximately four years later, she and her husband took over the pastorate of a small Baptist church in the one-stoplight town of Oden, Arkansas. A perfect "ministry couple," he preached while she sang and played the piano. The church grew quickly under their care. Over the next three years, the couple had two beautiful boys.

"That's when I learned that everything can seem fine on the outside, but that might not really be the case," Quita says.

In the fall of 1989, every aspect of Quita's life changed when out of the blue, her husband informed her that he wanted a divorce. With nothing but a high-school education, no money, and no car, Quita was suddenly faced with the responsibility of finding a job to provide for herself and the boys. It was a discouraging prospect that turned mortifying as a hoped-for job at the local bank never materialized. Instead, Quita was forced to accept the only position available to her at the time—a carhop for the town's popular drive-in eatery.

"You have to understand the small-town Sonic," Quita says. "Everyone goes there and knows everything about everyone.

"It felt as if people's eyes were burning my skin as I carried those trays. It was as if I could hear them say, 'There she is, the preacher's wife, whose husband divorced her.'"

Then one night as Quita walked out to deliver a tray of food, she froze as she realized her customer was her former husband. "I was humiliated," Quita says of that time, "but I held my head high."

"This can't be where You want me, Lord," she cried out on a cold January evening as she wearily picked up trash in the parking lot after closing. Immediately she sensed the Lord speak to her heart that she was exactly where He wanted her to be... for now.

As Quita learned to rest in God's provision and refused to allow bitterness to enter her heart, several things began to happen.

"I may have been the oldest carhop, but I was also the highest paid after I counted my tips each night," Quita reveals.

And as she swallowed her pride regarding government housing, it became clearly apparent that God had her there for a reason.

"Around midnight when I returned home from work one night, I found my pregnant neighbor along with her little boy, Scotty, from the duplex adjoining mine. They were crying on my front porch, because her husband had beaten her. She needed help, and because I was her neighbor, I was available for her.

"We were also surrounded by elderly neighbors who loved us and sort of adopted my boys as grandchildren. One particular Christian woman, Hazel, who lived next to us and was house-bound most of the time, spent a lot of time praying for us." In her humble surroundings, God had provided a place where Quita was both needed and loved.

As time passed, she found the pain and depression from the divorce lifting. She registered at the community college and began LPN classes while her children, Charley and Caleb, attended school. It was a difficult schedule, made possible only by loving friends and family and the grace of God. Reflecting back, Quita shares the secret of walking through that difficult season.

"As I was overcoming the depression and moving on with my life, an opportunity for bitterness began to show itself again. I quickly made the decision that I would not fall into that trap of the get-even, angry mode. Don't get me wrong, there were many times when it was tempting.

"Instead we focused on the fact that God had a plan for us—a good plan, like Jeremiah 29:11 NLT says: '"For I know the plans I have for you," says the Lord. "They are plans for good and not for disaster, to give you a future and a hope."' I decided to make the best of a hard situation."

At the same time God was healing Quita's heart, He was also at work in the heart of a quiet businessman in another state. The co-owner of a new business venture, Mike Feeley had never married. Now in his midtwenties, he had been praying over the last year for God to give him a wife with a couple of children. He began praying this specific prayer about the same time that Quita's husband had filed for divorce. Amazingly, even as Quita faced the devastation of her first marriage, God was already at work to restore.

With a little maneuvering by Quita's sister and Mike's sister–in–law, who through their friendship realized a potential match, Quita and Mike exchanged addresses. After several letters and phone calls, the two finally agreed to meet as Quita drove to Oklahoma to visit her sister.

"My heart was jumping like a young teenager on her first date!" Quita says. "Both of us were fairly quiet, but eventually we found ourselves talking like old friends. We realized in our hearts that we had not met by accident."

After that weekend, the letters and phone calls increased as did Quita's trips to her sister's house. What had seemed impossible just a year before was now unfolding quickly. God had given her a second chance at love.

On October 28, 1990, Mike and Quita married in a small wedding chapel. Since that time, Stephani and Jessica have joined Quita's two boys, and the bond between them all is supernatural.

One day after the girls were born, Quita sat down to have a serious talk with her two sons about their half sisters. She says, "I looked both of them in the eyes and said, 'Sometimes kids feel like their stepparent loves their own children more than their stepchildren. Do you guys ever feel this way?'

"I will never forget the amazed look on Charley's face as he proclaimed, 'I think he likes *us* the most.'

"That pretty well explains the kind of dad Mike is," Quita says.

"I reflect back on those dark days—the times when I was crying out to God, 'Where are You?' thinking He was nowhere to be found. Little did I know, He was busy preparing Mike's heart and our future. He who began a good work will be faithful to complete it in others, just as He has been faithful to complete it in us. (See Phil. 1:6.)

"I truly believe that a bitter heart would have blocked all of these blessings. But instead, I have children who don't wear the scars of divorce. I have been restored above and beyond anything I could have imagined. I thank the Lord for all that He has done in my life. And the good that has come from all the bad is being used to help others find hope in seemingly hopeless situations. Things don't always turn out the way we plan. Sometimes they turn out much better!"

God, I'm so thankful to be Your child because You take such good care of me. You see my life in its entirety and are constantly moving things around for my benefit. During those times when I can't see the forest for the trees, remind me to go up higher to where You are, so I can see things from Your perspective. Amen.

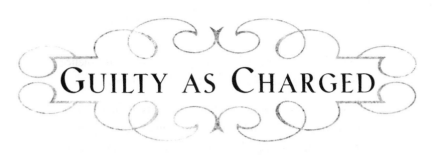

Guilty as Charged

[Jesus said], "If the Son sets you free, you will be free indeed."

John 8:36

Her hair hung over her eyes and face in tangled disarray. She left it there, a shield from the glaring eyes of her accusers. She wanted to crawl away from their taunting words. The bright sunlight exposed what she had tried to hide in the night.

Anger mixed with her shame as she noted the pious leaders who now stood condemning her. How dare they accuse her when some of the very men now surrounding her had called upon her for her services.

Is it any wonder they knew exactly where to find me? She berated herself for her carelessness.

The law was clear as to her punishment. Death.

Suddenly it all became clear. She wasn't whom they were really after. She was simply a pawn in their game as the religious leaders threw her as bait before the quiet rabbi. She studied his feet, unwilling to look him in the face. For the first time she noticed that he had bent down and seemed to be writing in the dirt. Why didn't he say something? His silence was almost worse than the accusations of the others.

As the leaders continued to hurl questions at the rabbi, he slowly stood to his feet and spoke with a quiet authority that silenced the noisy crowd, "If any one of you is without sin, let him be the first to cast a stone."

Eyeing the crowd, he once again stooped down and began to write.

She closed her eyes, waiting for the impact of the first stone. She had feared this day would come and wondered at her own stupidity. What did she have to show for her life? She had no husband. No security. No honor. She had nothing and was nothing—at all.

It is unclear how much time passed until the rabbi spoke again, his voice stirring her from her own thoughts, "Woman where are they? Has no one condemned you?"

Astonished, she slowly looked up. They were gone, all of them.

"No one, sir," she replied.

"Then neither do I condemn you," Jesus declared. "Go now and leave your life of sin."

That day was a new beginning. It was the woman's second chance at life and at love, and this time she was going to do it right.[13]

Life Lessons

1. Have you made a mistake that seems unforgiveable? While there are often consequences of our own making, forgiveness is always available when we come to God with a repentant heart. He is the God of second chances.
2. The guilt from past transgressions can create a prison without walls. God is eager to forgive you, but are you willing to forgive yourself?
3. God can take seeming disaster and turn the situation around for good.

[15] Story based upon John 8:1–11.

SECTION 7

Till Death Do Us Part

Love is like a friendship caught on fire.
In the beginning a flame, very pretty,
Often hot and fierce,
But still only light and flickering.
As love grows older,
Our hearts mature
And our love becomes as coals,
Deep-burning and unquenchable.

BRUCE LEE

THE LOVE OF A LIFETIME

FORMER FIRST LADY,

Nancy Reagan

I am my beloved's and my beloved is mine.

SONG OF SOLOMON 6:3 NASB

Her petite, aged hands stretched across the flag-draped coffin, smoothing the material as she might have smoothed out the wrinkles of his suit jacket. Patting the casket lovingly, Nancy Reagan turned her head and leaned close to whisper to the love of her life, seemingly oblivious to the millions who viewed the intimate scene. Bending down for a farewell kiss, her lips brushed the casket before turning back to her military escort. He then accompanied her out of the U.S. Capitol Rotunda, where fortieth president, Ronald Reagan, had lain in state for thirty-three hours. It was a moving display of their love, which spanned more than fifty years.

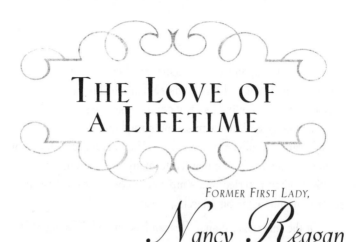

Nancy Davis met Ronald Wilson Reagan in 1951, when he was president of the Screen Actors Guild. At that time Reagan had been called upon by an industry producer to assist a young actress named Nancy Davis, whose name had mistakenly appeared on the mailing list of a communist newspaper. Reagan agreed to meet with the actress and straighten out the problem, giving Nancy a call a few days later. They arranged to meet for dinner, a chance meeting that led to many more evenings together. They married in a simple ceremony in Los Angeles several months later on March 4, 1952.

Of the marriage, Nancy Reagan has shared, "Though life was sometimes difficult [financially] in our early years together, Ronnie never let on that he was worried or upset. I knew he sometimes was—I just knew—but he never said anything outright. It just wasn't his way. Instead, he always tried to use humor to get through things....

"Like any other couple, we didn't agree on everything, of course. But we never really argued. We worked on things. And I think that's why, beyond our love for each other, our marriage has always been so happy. What we felt was right out there....

"I tried to explain this once in a letter to a woman in Washington, D.C., who was about to get married and had written to me in Sacramento to ask if I had any tips for building a good marriage. 'I'm very flattered that you wrote me, and I wish I thought I had a surefire formula for a successful marriage,' I wrote back.

"I've been very lucky. However, I don't ever remember once sitting down and mapping out a blueprint. It just became 'we' instead of 'I' very naturally and easily. And you live as you never have before, despite problems, separations and conflicts. I suppose mainly you have to be willing to want to give.... I can't imagine not being married to Ronnie. When two people really love each other they help each other stay alive and grow.... I suppose it boils down to being willing to try to understand, to give of yourself, to be supportive and not to let the sun go down on an argument."[14]

After his diagnosis of Alzheimer's disease in 1994, Nancy made the decision to share some of the letters she had received over the years in her book, *I Love You, Ronnie: The Letters of Ronald Reagan to Nancy Reagan.* The depth of their relationship is evidenced with note of their playful teasing, as well as tender devotion to each other. In one particular letter, Ronald Reagan expounded on his own definition of a wife.

"It means a companion without whom I'm never quite complete or happy. It means the most desirable woman in the world who gets more desirable every day. It means someone who can make me lonely just by leaving the room."[15]

In a letter to mark their thirty-first anniversary, written on Air Force One stationery, he notes that their marriage remains "an adolescent's dream of what marriage should be like.... When you aren't there I'm no place, just lost in time and space. I more than love you, I'm not whole without you."[16]

---

[14] Nancy Reagan, *I Love You, Ronnie: The Letters of Ronald Reagan to Nancy Reagan,* copyright © 2000 Ronald Reagan Presidential Foundation. Used by permission of Random House, Inc., pp. 38,104–105.

[15] Ibid., p. 131.

[16] Ibid., p. 162.

Of her position in the marriage and relationship, Nancy once commented to reporter Mike Wallace, "My job is being Mrs. Ronald Reagan."

Surprised, Wallace pressed her further, "Do you ever see yourself as a separate person?"

"No, I never do," she replied. "Always as Nancy Reagan. My life began with Ronnie."[17]

Then, just three months after their fifty-second anniversary, Ronald Reagan was gone, leaving his soul mate behind.

"This is a much different day for Nancy Reagan," stated Bob Schieffer, who, along with Dan Rather covered the final procession of the week-long state funeral, culminating with the private Reagan Library sunset service. "She is finally saying a good-bye that began ten years ago, from the man who has been the center of her life. Sometimes I want to look away from the strength that is there because I don't want to intrude on her grief. People may have said a lot of things about her as a first lady, but watching her now you have to say one thing about her. She loved the guy."[18]

Led by the hearse carrying Reagan's casket, the funeral procession made the long winding climb in the fading light of the

[17] Mike Wallace, CBS interview: *60 Minutes*, "The Reagan's Long Good-bye" http://www.cbsnews.com/stories/2002/09/24/60II/main523094.shtml. Accessed June 4, 2003.

[18] This account was taken from the CBS broadcast of Ronald Reagan's funeral, CBS Broadcasting Inc. June 11, 2004.

day to his final resting place. The world watched as Nancy Reagan stoically waved at the throngs of people who had lined the road.

CBS news correspondent Bill Plant reminisced of their unique relationship: "When you saw them together, it was as if there was no one else in the room or auditorium. As was their fashion, when they would greet an audience, they would stand holding hands and with their free hands turn and wave.... After they had been apart and would come back together, they would embrace and the rest of us might as well have been on Mars. So it is particularly poignant that she is now waving alone."[19]

Again and again throughout the procession, the strength, endurance, and special bond of the Reagan marriage was expressed. In the final moments of the sunset ceremony, the Reagan's pastor, Reverend Michael Wenning, turned to Mrs. Reagan and said, "Thank you for the example of your marriage, which you lived out before us—especially during the White House years.... Yours was truly a glorious friendship based on love and respect."[20]

The love, respect, and longevity of the Reagan marriage are the characteristics most notable in light of the tragic, ever-increasing divorce rate in the world today. The marriage vows, "for better or for worse, in sickness and in health," were

---

[19] Ibid., Bill Plant.

[20] Ibid., Reverend Michael Wenning.

stretched to their limit as Nancy Reagan walked with her husband through their final years together, a final chapter overshadowed by Alzheimer's disease. Although the malady ultimately robbed them of their most precious possessions—their memories and their ability to communicate with one another—it never robbed them of their love.

After the death of her father, Patti Davis said of the special bond between her parents, "In his last moment he taught me that there is nothing stronger than love between two people, two souls."[21]

Davis' parting words at the close of her father's funeral were made in reference to her parents' enduring love, even in the face of death: "I know that at his last moment, when [my father] opened his eyes, eyes that had not opened for many, many days, he showed us that neither disease nor death can conquer love.

"It was the last thing he could do to show my mother how entwined their souls are and it was everything."[22]

Theirs truly was the love of a lifetime—for all time.

God, You are the author of love stories. In fact, You have made me the object of Your love story. I am amazed when I realize that my face is ever before You and that I am always on Your mind. I affectionately honor and adore You, Lord. You are the lover of my soul, the love of my life. Amen.

---

[21] Ibid., Patti Davis.

[22] Ibid.

A Need Greater than My Own

Iru's Story

The LORD watches over the alien
and sustains the fatherless and the widow.

PSALM 146:9

It was 1974 when Iru received the call that her husband had been involved in a hunting accident. He died instantly, leaving behind his wife and three sons, the youngest twenty-two. With her children grown, Iru, only fifty years old, suddenly found herself all alone.

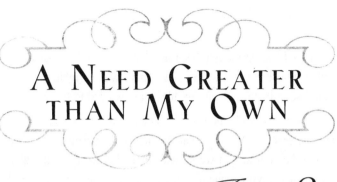

"My husband and I did everything together. We went to work together in the morning. We had lunch together. We even had coffee breaks together on most occasions since his office building adjoined the office where I worked," Iru says as she recounts the close relationship she shared with her husband. "After work we would then drive home together. For no particular reason, two years before his death, I had cut out all other activities I had previously been involved with and just spent time with my husband. He wasn't sick. There was no inkling that he would soon be taken from my life. I just wanted to be with him.

"After his death, the hardest thing for me to do was to go home after 5:00 P.M.," she shares. "Instead I determined to go to a nursing home nearby. I would walk up and down the halls talking with people, giving a hug to some and a listening ear to others. In my own pain, I began to reach out to others who had a need greater than my own. I soon found that after spending time giving to others, I was able to return to my own home with a peace that filled my heart, in spite of the void of my husband's presence."

Now, thirty years later, Iru is an integral part of the staff of her local church—which, incidentally, is pastored by one of her sons. There she has plenty of opportunities to share what she has learned.

She states, "Now when I talk with other widows, I encourage them to get involved with people as soon as they can. I know there is business to attend to, but after those things have been taken care of, I try to motivate them to get involved. It is important that they not focus on themselves, but stay active. This has helped me stay healthy and it will help others too."

Dear Lord, there are days when it seems that grief has settled upon my soul and all I can think about is my loss. As I reach out to others, whose needs are greater than my own, please heal my broken heart. Fill this void with Your peace and give me the grace to walk through this dark valley to brighter days ahead. Amen.

Twilight Love

The Story of

Ruth and Miles

The LORD God said, "It is not good for the man to be alone. I will make a helper suitable for him."

Genesis 2:18

The sun was beginning to set, casting an array of gold and orange hues across the cozy wedding chapel in the woods. I glanced around the room, searching for familiar faces, taking in the beautiful setting. Then I made an unusual discovery as I observed the individuals in the wedding party. They were all extremely young, ranging in age from as young as eight! A glance at the program revealed each person's unique relationship to the wedding couple. The photographers, the attendants, a musician, the ushers and hostesses were all related to the bride and the groom—they were their grandchildren!

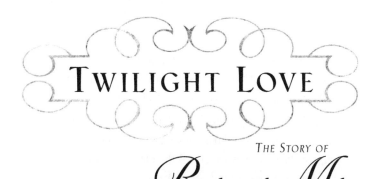

Both in their seventies, neither Ruth nor Miles thought they would ever marry again after experiencing the death of their spouses. Yet now, as they stood in the waning light in front of the minister to repeat their vows, they were about to embark on a delightful and unexpected chapter in their lives.

Jesse, Ruth's first husband, had battled and overcome several serious illnesses during his and Ruth's almost fifty years of marriage. First, it was cancer of the bladder and then colon cancer. However, two rounds of aggressive chemotherapy from these two diseases had taken their toll. The last diagnosis was leukemia, requiring weekly blood transfusions. The six- to eight-hour procedures turned the skin on Jesse's arm varying shades of black and blue from his wrist to his elbow. As the disease progressed, his body needed the transfusions with greater and greater frequency.

As the need increased, so did the length of the hospital stays. Ruth would stay by Jesse's side during his sometimes two-week confinement, often returning home only long enough to shower and change clothes.

It was an exhausting schedule for both Ruth and the entire family who rallied together. The close-knit unity of Ruth's family was unmistakable. Jesse's doctor even commented from his observations, "I've seen lots of families over the years, but none quite as devoted as yours." It was with the help of her loving family that Ruth buried her husband just shy of their fiftieth wedding anniversary.

As time passed, Ruth gradually began to fill her schedule with activities at her church and in the community, as well as by spending time with her children, grandchildren, and great-grandchildren. Slowly, she recovered from her grief, and life was good. Naturally, she missed Jesse, but Ruth was content.

Miles and his wife were no strangers to Ruth's family. The couple had often come to the hospital to visit during Jesse's many stays there. Miles had been a pastor in Kansas for twenty-six years before moving to Oklahoma. It didn't take long before he was asked to join the staff as a "care pastor" of the large church that both families attended. He and his wife, Carol, made a good team as he ministered to the five hundred families under his care and his wife handled the enormous administrative aspect of the position. It was Miles and Carol who were the first to arrive at the hospital after Jesse's death to comfort the family.

Approximately three years later, Miles went through an experience similar to Ruth's as his wife battled lymphoma. After her death, Miles continued to stay active, becoming a chaplain at the Cancer Treatment Center where his wife had been treated and performing numerous weddings and funerals each month. Ministering to others helped him through the grieving process.

One evening Miles called Ruth to chat.

"I never gave it much thought," Ruth comments. "I thought he was simply operating in his role as a pastor and checking up on me."

But when Miles called a week later and invited Ruth out for dessert, the realization hit. He was asking her out on a date!

The two began attending activities together and went to lunch on occasion, both enjoying their growing friendship. "I never thought about marrying again," Ruth shares. "After all, I had been a widow more than six years and felt quite content. Besides, I always thought that even if I were interested in someone, he would never be interested in me."

Ruth remembers a conversation she had with Miles as they were sitting together on her porch swing one evening. "I was telling Miles how content I was at being alone, trying to encourage him that it gets easier over time." Misunderstanding Miles' intention, Ruth thought he was still grieving.

"Good one, Mom," her daughter laughed about the incident later. "If he was interested in you, you just blew it."

"I'm not trying to find a boyfriend," Ruth defended her actions.

Ruth may not have been looking for a boyfriend for herself, but she learned later that her kids were!

Christmas Eve had always been a time of special family traditions for her family as they gathered to unwrap packages and listen to old tunes. Only this year, one of Ruth's daughters had a special surprise. Unbeknownst to Ruth, she had invited Miles to join them! And he fit right in.

After that Miles and Ruth began to see each other with increasing frequency. She attended the weddings he performed, and he would come over to join her for a home-cooked meal. Over time, Ruth noticed a change in their conversation as Miles began making comments about when they would marry.

"How do you know that I *would* marry you?" Ruth countered after one such comment.

Miles was quiet for a moment before answering, "Well, *will* you marry me?" he finally popped the question.

Ruth accepted, but the couple dated for another entire year before even setting a date, just to ensure that the foundation they were building upon was solid.

"My oldest daughter called me one day," Ruth recalls. "She was the one who had secretly invited Miles to our Christmas celebration, so I think that she was behind the relationship all along. In any event she tried to help us speed up the process and told me, 'Mom, if you're going to marry him, you better set a date!'"

Miles was now seventy; and Ruth, well, a woman never tells her age, but let's just say that Miles has always preferred older women. Following her daughter's advice, the couple set a date and married this past March.

As I visit with the couple, the love and friendship that they share is unmistakable as Miles comments on Ruth's beauty and gentle nature and she replies with a similar loving remark.

"Ronald Reagan once said of Nancy that the moment she stepped out of a room, loneliness stepped in. That is how I feel about Ruth," Miles reinforces.

To listen to them and watch them together, you might think they were young teens experiencing first love, but their union is a testimony that true love can happen to anyone at any age.

Heavenly Father, You are so kind and good to bring romantic love into the lives of widows and widowers. But regardless of my age or marital status, You love me with an everlasting love. Thank You for godly relationships when I am lonely and for comforting me during times of grief. Lead me to those whom I might encourage, so that I might be a blessing to others. Amen.

I WILL NOT LEAVE

Don't be selfish; don't live to make a good impression on others. Be humble, thinking of others as better than yourself. Don't just think about your own affairs, but be interested in others, too.

PHILIPPIANS 2:3–4 TLB

"Where you die, I will die; and there I will be buried. May the Lord deal with me, be it ever so severely, if anything but death separates you and me," said Ruth.

Such strong words from a young woman—not toward the man she loved, but to...her mother-in-law?

After the death of her husband, followed by the deaths of both of her sons ten years later, Naomi instructed her two daughters-in-law to return to their families.

"You are young and I am old," she began. "I cannot provide you with another husband. In fact, I have nothing to offer you," Naomi explained bitterly. "Go."

The three women, bound by shared tragedy, wept together at their loss. Then, as reality set in, the first daughter-in-law took Naomi's advice and returned to her family. Her departure only highlighted Ruth's selfless act. Essentially, Ruth extended the vow she had made to her husband to include his mother. Ruth refused to leave Naomi, but chose rather to remain faithful to her until death.

On the surface, Ruth's sacrificial decision not to return to her own family looked as if it would cost her everything. But, in fact, all that she had lost was restored to her and more as the wealthy landowner Boaz asked her to marry him. Pure love, so rarely seen, attracts attention and brings great reward, because it seeks none.[23]

Life Lessons

1. Love, in covenant form, is not only a decision, but an act of the will. It seeks not its own pleasure, but rather the good of the one loved. True love is willing to sacrifice; it is committed to walk through the most difficult circumstances unmoved and unwavering.
2. Many seek true love, yet are unwilling to sacrifice their comfort to attain such a treasure. Yet, without sacrifice, love remains in infancy, unable to reach the depth of fulfillment that the heart craves.
3. God always rewards true love.

[23] Story based upon the book of Ruth.

Uncommon Love

Love feels no burden, thinks nothing of trouble, attempts what is above its strength, pleads no excuse of impossibility; for it thinks all things lawful for itself, and all things possible. It is therefore able to undertake all things, and warrants them to take effect, where he who does not love, would faint and lie down.

THOMAS À KEMPIS

SECTION 8

The Power of Love

Love has power to give in a moment
what toil can scarcely reach in an age.

JOHANN WOLFGANG VON GOETHE

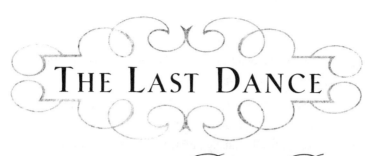

The Last Dance

Renée Bondi

AS TOLD TO KAREN HARDIN

I was pushed back and about to fall,
but the LORD helped me.
The LORD is my strength and my song;
he has become my salvation.

PSALM 118:13–14

I called Renée at the appointed time for our scheduled interview. "Can you give me about thirty minutes?" she asked. "The carpenter is here and things are just a little hectic. If you can give me about thirty minutes, I think I can get things under control."

When we reconnected thirty minutes later, Renée was warm and friendly, even if a little frazzled from her chaotic morning. In the midst of remodeling, as well as working on a schedule for her assistant, not to mention the work regarding her speaking ministry, it sounded very much like a typical morning in the life of a busy lady. Only Renée's life is anything but typical. This is her story.

"All right, I'll go out with him," I finally conceded to my friend, Rosie. *How bad can it be? It's just a dinner?* I thought to myself, hoping that by finally giving in to Rosie's persistent request, it would put the matter behind us.

Rosie and her fiancé, Greg, were perpetual matchmakers. For the last three years, they had tenaciously worked to get me and their mutual friend Mike out on a blind date. For a while, I was able to push off their attempts with the excuse that I was already involved in a dating relationship, but Rosie wasn't fooled. She knew, as well as I did, that I needed to end that relationship. And once I finally did, she started back up with a vengeance. I didn't learn until later that Mike was dragging his heels as much as I.

Finally, just to get them to stop, I agreed to meet Mike. Interestingly, at the exact same time, Mike had finally made the same determination—willing to meet me so that the issue would finally be settled, once and for all.

Our foursome went to dinner together one Sunday night after attending Mass. It was actually an enjoyable dinner during which Rosie and Greg took great delight in pointing out our many similarities. I had to admit that Mike was easy to get along with, but the truth of the matter was, there were absolutely no sparks indicating a love interest. We said good-bye that night, not even exchanging phone numbers.

Seven months later I saw Mike again at Greg and Rosie's wedding. Since neither of us knew very many at the wedding, we often found ourselves together on the dance floor. I loved to dance and the evening passed quickly as he held me in his arms. This time he got my phone number and used it often. Many romantic dinners and long walks on the beach followed until we became engaged two years later.

When Mike proposed, I remember him pulling out a little wooden box in the shape of a heart. My stomach began to do flip-flops with a sense of anticipation. Inside the small velvet-lined container was a beautiful teardrop sapphire necklace surrounded by small diamonds. "I thought it would be nice if we picked out the ring together," he shared. "Will you marry me?"

I started to cry and immediately said, "Yes." This was the man I wanted to spend the rest of my life with. We set a date for July the following year.

Two months before our wedding, Mike and I were to be chaperones for the San Clement High senior prom. I think I was as excited as my students, as I got ready for the special event. Before the prom, Mike took me to one of our favorite restaurants, The Velvet Turtle. I could tell by the look on his face that something was up. During the meal, he pulled a small box out of his pocket and slipped onto my finger the ring we had picked out. As I watched it sparkle in the light, I felt that things couldn't possibly get any better.

The rest of the evening, between checking out the bath-rooms in our role as chaperones, we danced and talked of our impending marriage. We had no idea the postponements and the battle that lay before us.

The following night I conducted the orchestra for our school's spring musical. It had been a wonderful evening. I went to bed late that night and before drifting off to sleep, relished in the thought of how blessed I was to have a job I enjoyed and a man I loved.

However, I awoke abruptly in the middle of the night—and found myself in midair! Landing on my head, my feet flipped over me and I lay sprawled on the floor. As I attempted to rise, I heard my neck crack and an excruciating wave of pain flooded over me. I couldn't get up; and worse yet, when I attempted to call for help, my voice came out in a weak whisper.

Miraculously, my roommate awakened at the exact same moment and came to check on me, something she had never done before.

"I can't get up," I croaked. "Call the paramedics."

Once in the emergency room, doctors fought to save my life. I still had no idea how extensive my injuries were, after all I had only gone to bed. "How did you fall?" I was asked repeatedly, but I had no answer. I had no idea what had happened. I didn't try to move because my previous attempt had brought severe, throbbing pain. But I never imagined I *couldn't* move. But the next morning, the doctors confirmed the worst as they viewed the X rays of my injury. My neck was broken and I would never walk again.

During the dark days that followed, I was amazed by Mike's commitment to me. For him it wasn't a matter of wondering if he would still marry me, rather, would I survive so that we could still have a life together? Mike was there with me every day along with my family, encouraging me and holding my hand.

It took a month before I was out of the woods and five more for my condition to stabilize. The months that followed were spent adjusting to the new set of circumstances before us. Neither one of us had bargained for this. And we had no idea what to expect.

Six months after I was released from the hospital, Mike proposed...again.

"Are you serious?" I asked. "How could you want to marry me this way?"

"Your mind, your personality, and your heart have not changed, Renée. It is only your body that has changed. I still love you."

So we married in October of 1989, one year after I was released from the hospital. Mike and I may have danced our last dance, but it wasn't our last song.

MIKE AND RENÉE BONDI make their home in southern California with their nine-year-old son, Daniel. To learn more about Renée or to have her speak for your organization, contact: www.reneebondi.com.

Heavenly Father, Your unconditional love and acceptance are greater than anything I can fathom. Thank You for raising up people to express Your love to me when I need it. And I pray that You will use me to encourage and minister to others who are hurting. Thank You for Your uncommon and gracious love. Amen.

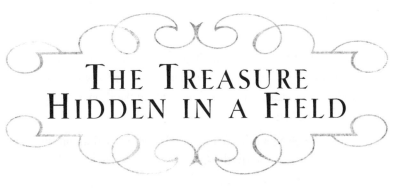

The Treasure Hidden in a Field

In your distress you called and I rescued you.

Psalm 81:7

Carefully dressing their infant son in the beautiful yellow silk outfit, the parents then tucked a ten-dollar bill under his arm for his passage to the next life. After laying their precious bundle in the field, they turned and walked away forever.

The baby, approximately six weeks old, had been burned over 80 percent of his body. His left side, which received the worst of the accident, was completely charred. Deep burns lined his chin and mouth along with his stomach, feet, and right hand. The silky material, what was to be his burial outfit, was soon stained by his own body fluids, adhering the once-beautiful material to his little body.

The tiny child was still alive when a local villager found him. The kindly man took the baby to the unschooled village doctor; however, the village leadership confirmed that the wounds were far too serious for them to treat. They recommended that he be taken to the local state-run orphanage.

"The first time I saw him, he stole my heart," shares Lisa Bentley of the Philip Hayden Foundation, an orphanage established by Americans Tim and Pam Baker in the People's Republic of China.

"We received a call from the local farm hospital in our city that a baby had just arrived who had been severely burned. They asked us if we wanted him.

"When I walked into the hospital a short while later, it struck me that although the child was in critical condition, he had no mommy who would be fighting to get him the best care possible." Lisa made an immediate decision in her heart that she would fight for this baby. She would be the mother he didn't have.

Lisa and her husband, John, had only been in China three months when they received the call that night from the hospital, but the events that had led them to be in China in the first place were extraordinary.

For three years, they followed God's call for John to go to law school. Lacking adequate financial means, their faith was encouraged by the story of George Müller, a famous British citizen who had helped thousands of orphans in Britain in the 1800s. George Müller never asked for money and always trusted God to meet his needs and the needs of the many orphans in his care.

John thought, *If George could do it, I can do it.* After three years of law school, God had provided manna from Heaven—approximately one hundred thousand dollars—to support their family and pay for law school tuition. The money always came from different sources and on many occasions at the eleventh hour; but in the end, John graduated without any student loans.

Toward the end of his third year of law school, John and Lisa were talking and praying one day about where they thought God would lead them when he graduated. In the background, the radio was playing, set on a local Christian station. At the time, the host was interviewing the director of a mission organization to China. As the interview came to a close, the host ended by asking the mission director what they needed most. Although John was not really paying attention to the radio interview, the next words leaped out at him.

His answer was not for prayer or finances, things you might expect. What they *most* needed were people with a Juris Doctor or MBA degree. John was stunned. He had *both* of those degrees. Sensing that this might be the direction that he and Lisa had just been praying for, John called the organization later that day. They were very excited to talk to John, but their program was designed to send Christian business and legal experts to teach in Chinese universities. The program required nine months of training—across the country, at no pay. After three years of law school, this simply was not an option for John and Lisa. With two children, they needed a job. John was disappointed, but the seed had been planted. God began powerfully working in his heart to go to China—if not this way, then another.

After graduating from law school, John took a job with a law firm as he prepared for the final stage, his bar exam.

Always expecting to work as a prosecuting attorney, he was surprised when God began to speak to his heart about going to China. Not knowing what that would mean, John took the exam and waited expectantly for the results.

"Your name is not on the list," the clerk informed John when he called for his exam results.

"I couldn't believe it," John exclaims. "I kept thinking, *God, why did You tell me to go to law school, knowing that I would fail the bar exam? It doesn't make sense.*"

But without the legal credentials forthcoming, John was laid off from his firm. Now the bigger question was, how was he going to provide for his family?

Out of the blue, he received a call from the organization that he had heard on the radio months earlier. One of their professors who had been scheduled to teach a law and a business course had had to leave China early. John was the only person they had on file who had a background in both.

"You wouldn't happen to be available to go to China would you? We will pay your expenses to come," the caller encouraged.

John and Lisa, remembering what God had already spoken to their hearts about China, agreed on the brief separation so that John could accept the short-term position. In doing so, he would become an answer to an urgent prayer.

John had only been working in China for six weeks when he received a call from a lady with the accent of a New Zealander.

"Are you the American lawyer, John Bentley?" the woman asked. "I know you don't know me, but I have to tell you, God sent you here to help me."

John listened as the woman shared of her struggle to complete the lengthy legal forms necessary for her to establish her Chinese orphan care center in Guangzhou. In her words, she explained that she was just a "mum." In frustration, she had called out to God, saying that she could not do this alone. She needed a lawyer to help her. But where would she find a Western, Christian lawyer in southern China?

"Lord, I can't fill out these forms," she finally exclaimed. "Please send me someone who can."

"He told me He already had," the woman informed John. "And you are the man."

John was amazed that the woman had even found him.

He agreed to help and a time was set for him to assist with the needed project.

A week later, the phone rang in John's apartment, waking him at the stroke of midnight. *Who could be calling at this hour of the night,* he wondered?

"Is this John Bentley, Esquire?" Lisa asked playfully. Unable to contain herself, Lisa immediately continued. "There was a mistake, John, you *did* pass the bar exam!"

John sat up as he absorbed the information. He *was* a lawyer! But had he not been led to believe that he had failed the exam, he wouldn't have been in China at that very moment to help the lady from New Zealand. As John looked at his watch, he marveled over God's timing. It was one minute past midnight, Christmas Day...an incredible gift.

Shortly afterward, John returned to the States to be with his family and took a job with a prestigious law firm in Washington state. For the next four years, he worked his way up the ladder, marking numerous achievements along the way. John was now working for the largest law firm in Vancouver, making a good salary and doing what he had been trained to do. Only John and Lisa weren't happy.

"God, if this is all there is, it stinks," Lisa remembers saying, as she was pregnant with their fourth child. They had a new home, a new sports car, bonuses, and raises. They had achieved the American dream. They should have been content—but they weren't. They both longed for fulfillment...to use their lives to make a difference in the world around them.

That inner stirring was simply preparing them for an encounter with Philip Hayden Foundation founders, Tim and Pam Baker, who had started an orphanage in China. The more they learned of the incredible needs of the orphans in that country, John and Lisa finally made the difficult decision to uproot their family and go to China on a three-month trial basis.

Friends and family were not supportive of this decision and suggested that it would end in disaster. One could hardly blame them. The Philip Hayden Foundation is an all-volunteer organization. The Bentleys would be leaving the safety and security of his salary as a lawyer and stepping out in faith, believing that

God would supply their needs as they followed Him, just as He had while John was in law school. Lisa was particularly skeptical, but agreed to go and test the waters. If, after three months, she was not convinced that they had made the right decision, she could veto the idea and they would return to America and the practice of law.

The first two months in China were indeed difficult. The Bentleys had very little financial support, were living in a rodent-infested house with no heat in the dead of winter, with no car of their own. Despite these hardships, Lisa knew that they were needed in China. Two months into their stay, Lisa knew that they were meant to be in China, but she still wasn't happy about it. She asked Tim and John to pray for her that God would give her a heart for the people of China. Within two weeks, God honored that prayer through the life of a child.

Standing next to the tiny infant, struggling for his life, Lisa felt her heart change. This baby needed a mom to love and fight for him, although it looked like he wouldn't live long.

After being transferred to Beijing's children's hospital, a doctor there questioned, "Why do you want to save this baby's life? Look at him. What kind of life can he have? Why not just let nature take its course?"

"Listen, if no one else wants this baby, if no one else will adopt this baby, I will adopt him," stated Tim Baker, director of the Philip Hayden Foundation.

With an exploding population of 1.3 billion people in China, the life of one small burned baby held little value to the Chinese staff. They didn't mean to be cruel, just unnervingly pragmatic.

"Do whatever you can," Tim told them. "It doesn't matter how much money it costs."

"Once we put value on Levi's life, they began to value his life too," Tim recalls.

Prior to surgery, Lisa was presented with legal forms releasing the hospital from responsibility. The doctors explained that Levi would not survive the surgery. He was too young and his burns too extensive. His chance of survival was extremely slim.

"If this baby survives, it will be your God who saves him," one of the doctors told Lisa.

Lisa called John to say that she would be spending the night with Levi at the hospital. If this was to be his last night on the earth, she did not want him to be alone. She sat by his incubator, reading the Bible to him and cooing at him. Levi became quiet as he looked into her eyes and listened to her voice while trying to suck his little burned thumb. It broke Lisa's heart.

Although Chinese hospitals are dilapidated, dimly lit, and depressing places, Lisa's time with Levi was rich. As she read from the Bible, it came alive. One of the passages she was led to was Psalm 118:

> When I was in great pain, I cried out to the LORD.
> He answered me and set me free.

The LORD is with me. I will not be afraid....
I was pushed back. I was about to be killed.
But the LORD helped me...
"The LORD's powerful right hand has won the battle!
The LORD's powerful right hand has done mighty things!"
I will not die. I will live.
I will talk about what the LORD has done.

Verses 5–6,13,16–17 NIRV

Another verse that stood out was Matthew 13:44, which says: "The kingdom of Heaven is like treasure hidden in a field." She had the powerful impression that God was affirming that His kingdom existed not in buildings or organizations, but in the demonstration of love and mercy to this orphan. In God's eyes and in theirs, he was a treasure that had been hidden in a field.

During the first surgery, the doctors had to amputate the toes on Levi's left foot as well as his left arm from the wrist down. "There was so little undamaged skin available for grafting that the surgeons had to take skin from the top of his head to patch his small body," Lisa reveals. To the doctors' surprise, Levi survived the surgery.

"Since he is still alive, we are going to have to perform further skin graft surgery," the doctors informed the Bentleys.

"We have never had a baby so young and so severely burned survive," one of the doctors later informed Lisa. Blood loss, shock, and infection were just a few of the numerous complications that should have already resulted in his death, yet the little guy was still holding on.

As is common with burn victims, another infection developed and the doctors raced Levi back into surgery. This time they had to amputate the left arm further up past the elbow.

As Levi was fighting for his life, another fight was underway to obtain the necessary paperwork, so he could be brought to America for treatment at the Shriner's pediatric burn hospital in Boston. The Chinese medical professionals had done all they could, but it was not enough. The Shriners, widely recognized as one of the top burn centers in the world, agreed to perform the rest of his surgeries for free—if they could find a way to get him to America.

As news of the young baby traveled through the community, others rallied on Levi's behalf to assist in the effort for his survival. For Levi to leave China required that he obtain a Chinese passport as well as a difficult to obtain visa from the U.S. embassy in Beijing. Bureaucratic processes that would normally take months were accomplished almost overnight as officials from both governments worked together to get Levi all the papers he needed for travel to the U.S.

The only thing that still blocked their path was the needed plane tickets. Then, just as it seemed that victory was within their grasp, Levi developed yet another infection. His frail frame couldn't seem to overcome the constant fever, which racked his body. Time was running out. Lisa began calling airlines from different countries, trying to find someone who would donate tickets to help them. Every airline turned her down until she contacted United Airlines. Within an hour, the next miracle had occurred as the agent confirmed that United Airlines would provide them three round-trip business-class tickets from Beijing to Boston. They would leave in twenty-four hours.

"Lisa, where are you going to stay once you are in Boston?" her husband questioned realistically.

"I don't know, but I can see that God has parted the sea for us. I know that He loves us and will provide for all our needs as He always has," Lisa told her husband with confidence.

As Lisa; her eight-year old daughter, Emily; and Levi entered the plane the next day, Lisa had only fifty dollars to last through the trip. But again, God provided through a series of miracles and friendly strangers.

As we prepared to transfer planes after the first leg of the journey, a Chinese businesswoman handed us one hundred dollars. On the next plane, a flight attendant came up to us and handed us another twenty dollars.

"I don't make much money, but I want to give you this," she stated.

Throughout the next few days, Lisa was given even more money by complete strangers whose lives were touched by the plight of little Levi.

"Although I had no idea where we would stay in Boston, I could already see His provision," Lisa remembers.

Lisa might not have been as confident had she known at the time that they would be arriving in Boston the weekend of the famous Boston Marathon. Practically every hotel in the city was completely booked! But Lisa was not in this alone. People all over the world were praying and trying to help. Lisa's longtime friend, Traci Nelson from Washington state, began calling hotels in Boston, explaining the situation and trying to find a hotel that would sponsor them. Finally, the Holiday Inn Select, right next door to Shriner's Hospital, agreed to provide them a room, free of charge, for the duration of their stay in Boston. When she called Lisa to give her the good news, she had other startling news as well.

"Lisa, I have chills. Do you realize that Levi's name in Hebrew means 'to bind and unite together'?" Although he was just a two-month-old infant, Levi had already been used by God to bind together and unite people, companies, and governments all over the world.

Arriving at the hospital, Lisa, Levi, and Emily were met enthusiastically.

"We've been waiting three weeks for this baby to get here!" the staff at the Shriner's Burn Hospital said as they immediately unwrapped Levi's wounds and began work.

Since Levi would be in intensive care for at least the next two months, Lisa and Emily were now faced with the task of finding foster parents during his hospital stay since they would have to return to China. The day before Lisa was to leave, she received a phone call that would lead her to that very special couple.

Linda and Don Evans had heard about Levi through their pastor. Instantly they knew they were to play a part in this miracle story. Although they lived an hour from the Shriner's Hospital, Linda made the trip every day during the next two months as Levi underwent several more surgeries and physical therapy.

"Once we met Levi, it was kind of like all of the other things we had to take care of didn't seem important," Don shares.

When Levi was finally able to be released from the hospital, Linda and Don were right there to take him to their home and love him back to health.

"Levi has brought so many people together," states Linda.

And that is exactly what baby Levi has done as Americans and Chinese, believers and unbelievers, worked diligently to save his life. As we talk, Lisa refers to the hundreds of e-mails they have received from people all over the world who have learned of his story and have been praying for his survival. At less than six months old, Levi had already touched the lives of more people than some do in their entire lives. God's hand is obviously upon him.

On February 14, 2005, Levi will be three years old. Sadly doctors have had to remove his left arm just above his elbow, all his fingers except a thumb, and several toes due to the severity of his burns. He almost lost his left foot as well. But none of that slows down this exceptional little boy. He not only walks, but also loves to race with the other children. "He can get into more trouble with his one thumb than if he had all ten fingers!" Lisa exclaims.

After three months in the States, Levi was released from the hospital and able to return to China.

"Levi is a very rare person who has been able to touch people all over the world," John Bentley shares. Born to peasants in the harshest conditions, his parents left him in the field, not because they didn't love him, but because they had no money to help him."

When Lisa Bentley prayed that night for God to give her a heart for China, little did she realize that God would answer that prayer by giving her a very special son.

God, You are amazing as You coordinate people, governments, institutions, and time to achieve Your will. Nothing is too difficult for You, and I trust You with my whole heart. Thank You for seeing the big picture and for working all things out for my good. Thank You for answering me when I call. Amen.

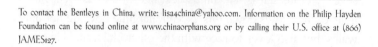

To contact the Bentleys in China, write: lisa4china@yahoo.com. Information on the Philip Hayden Foundation can be found online at www.chinaorphans.org or by calling their U.S. office at (866) JAMES127.

CARRIED THROUGH THE STORM

Wilma's Story

The LORD is my strength and my song;
he has become my salvation.

EXODUS 15:2

At an age when many women are looking forward to retirement and a time to enjoy the fruits of years of labor, Wilma found herself instead being the caregiver of her adult daughter as well as struggling with her own failing health. She was only nineteen when she had Cherree, her only child. She and her husband, Gene, never dreamed of the horrific circumstances that would unfold as their daughter made choices that would have tragic and irreversible consequences.

"Cherree was seventeen and pregnant when she ran away from home more than thirty years ago now. For a year, we had no idea where she was or if she was okay. Shortly after she left, her boyfriend, Lee, came over to our home to speak to me," Wilma recounts quietly.

"'Is she okay?' I asked, trying to remain calm. I had asked the Lord to help me love this young man, but it was very difficult as he stood there before me, unwilling to tell me where my own daughter was staying," Wilma admits.

With no way to contact Cherree, Wilma did the only thing she could do and that was to pray. Often she would wake up in the middle of the night to pray for an hour or more for her young daughter and the grandchild who would soon be born. One night as she was praying, she felt so heavy inside that all she could do as she knelt on the floor beside their couch was call out her name, "Cherree, Cherree, Cherree." Wilma learned later that at about that same time, her daughter was in Illinois sitting on *her* sofa and heard her mother calling her, *Cherree, Cherree, Cherree.* Yet she still didn't contact her parents.

One cold winter morning when Wilma got up early to pray, Cherree was again heavy on her heart. Looking out the kitchen window into the darkness, Wilma's heart was frantic with worry, *Where is she?* It was all she could think about.

"As I stood in the quiet early morning, God spoke clearly to my heart," Wilma remembers. "*She's in My care.* It was so strong and clear that from that moment on, I was able to rest and entrust her to God. It was almost a year later before she finally contacted us through one of her girlfriends and arranged a time that she would call me."

When the call came, Wilma cried for the first five to ten minutes of the conversation. She was so overjoyed to hear her daughter's voice. During the conversation, she learned that she had a six–month–old granddaughter named Denise and that Cherree wanted to come home.

"I was shocked when one morning they came into the drugstore where I worked," Wilma said. "She was holding the cutest little girl I had ever seen with naturally curly blond hair that hung to her shoulders and the most beautiful big blue eyes that reminded me of Tweety Bird. Lee, Cherree's boyfriend, was with them."

"'Mom, I don't know what Dad is going to think when he sees us,' Cherree began. 'He'll probably be mad,' she finished in a half question, half statement.

"'Your guess is as good as mine,' I answered, unsure how my husband would respond to our prodigal daughter's return.

"Cherree and her father had always been exceptionally close, so her disappearance had been especially difficult for him. He had already had a slight heart attack in his early thirties, and Cherree was concerned how their return might affect him."

As they arrived at the house, the four went in through the back kitchen door. Gene, who happened to be off work that day, was standing at the stove with his back to them.

"Dad," Cherree called out. Gene turned at the sound of her voice, too stunned to speak. "I've waited a long time for you to meet your granddaughter."

Still silent Gene took the baby in his arms as the nine–month–old wrapped her tiny arms around his neck and lay on his shoulder.

They all stood there in silence, not sure what would happen, but then the baby raised up her head and looked her grandfather straight in the face and just smiled. Her sweet face seemed to communicate what Cherree so far had been unable to, asking for his acceptance and forgiveness.

"That was when I noticed a tear trickle down his face," says Wilma. "Then Cherree walked up to him and putting her arms around him said, 'Dad, please forgive me.' Right behind her was Lee with an outstretched arm.

"I hope you will shake hands with me," Lee said. "But if you don't, I will understand."

As Gene reached for the offered hand, the distance that had separated their family for so long began to evaporate as God began to heal the wounds inflicted on the relationship. Cherree and Lee got married a year later and their son, Scooter, joined the family when Denise was four. If they could have ended the story there, things would have been "happily ever after." Unfortunately that wasn't the case.

Not long after this, Cherree and Lee made some new friends who turned them on to dope. Everything went downhill from there.

"Once I learned of the drug use, I would often go to check on the kids," Wilma shares in a voice that still trembles with the frustration she had felt. "Sometimes Lee wouldn't let me into the house. He wouldn't even tell me how they were doing. Other times I would go in to find Denise having to fill the role of an adult, single-handedly taking care of her little brother. At one point, I learned that Cherree had slit her wrists as the drug use escalated. I never knew when I went over if she would be dead or alive. In desperation I asked Cherree if I could take the kids and raise them, but she wouldn't let me."

As the drug use increased, the money decreased. Unable to pay their bills, Cherree and Lee moved from one apartment complex to another when they were routinely evicted. By the time Denise turned sixteen, she escaped her horrible home condition, got a job, and rented her own apartment.

"I wanted her to stay with me," Wilma explains, but she wouldn't. She married a couple of years later, but the marriage didn't last long."

It was about that time that Gene and Wilma moved to a smaller town in the same state. With their move, Wilma had a plan.

"I think we should try to get the kids to move down here with us. They might be able to get their lives together here in a smaller town," she told her husband.

Amazingly, Cherree, Lee, and Scooter, now eighteen, moved in with Wilma and Gene. They stayed a year, but it was a difficult situation as Gene was gone on an out-of-state construction job, leaving Wilma to deal with a critical son-in-law and rebellious grandson. As the situation continued to deteriorate, Gene and Wilma took action, paying the first month's rent for a small apartment for Cherree and her family.

"They wanted us to sign for their utilities as well, but I finally told her, 'No, honey. You are on your own now. I've done all I can do.'"

Cherree and Lee didn't pay the rent and reentered their previous cycle of eviction and moving until one day Wilma called to talk with Cherree and found she was very sick.

"I didn't know what was wrong at the time," Wilma said. "But it seemed like she and Lee were both always sick. This continued for two or three years when finally my brother-in-law said to us, 'You know, it's difficult to say this, but I think they both have AIDS.'

"I later learned that Gene had already suspected the same," says Wilma. "But with my brother-in-law's words, he gained the courage to confront Lee and Cherree regarding their prolonged illness."

"I'm so sorry, Dad," Cherree admitted that fateful day as Wilma and Gene finally learned the truth.

Without hesitation Gene responded, "I still love you, honey, and will stick with you until the end."

Not long after, Cherree and Lee agreed to attend a revival service in the area. At that service, Cherree gave her heart to the Lord, but Lee showed no sign of change. As their health continued to fail, Denise stepped in and she and Wilma took turns taking care of them.

"I remember about a week or so after the revival service, Lee was walking the short distance to the laundry room of the small apartment complex where they lived. I watched him as he returned to the apartment so frail and weak. 'I have to know if you're ready to meet God,' I said to him when he returned. 'You have a choice. It's either Heaven or hell. But it's my desire to meet you in Heaven.'"

Lee slowly raised his head and looked Wilma straight in the face before saying, "I'm ready." He died at home three weeks later, just fifty-one years old.

After Lee's death, Wilma and Gene moved Cherree to their home, but it quickly proved to be more than they could handle. Finally, they rented a small apartment for her, where once again Denise and Wilma took turns taking care of her. But as Cherree's condition continued to worsen, she was eventually hospitalized and then put in a rest home for more constant care. The strain of the past several years had begun to take their toll on Wilma, and her own health began to decline.

"It was so difficult to see my daughter in that condition," Wilma confesses. "She probably weighed only eighty pounds and was usually heavily sedated to keep her out of pain. I remember attending a prayer meeting during that time in which I felt such a weight for Cherree.

"'Lord, I know You can heal her, but would she walk with You?' I remember praying that night. 'Lord, I don't know how to pray, so I commit her to You. But let me turn her loose when I am ready.'"

As Wilma sat in prayer, she remembers sensing God's Spirit coming upon her as He spoke to her heart, *Don't look at what you see, look beyond.*

I'm just upset, Wilma remembers thinking to herself, and yet three different times that evening, the Lord spoke the same words to her. *Don't look at what you see, look beyond.*

Cherree died a few days later.

"When I look back, I am amazed at what happened during that difficult season," Wilma shares. "I had one particularly close friend who had been praying with me through the years. After Cherree died, I felt like something good came over me and I knew I could make it. Even during the funeral, my sister turned to me and asked, 'Are you okay?'

"'I'm fine,' I told her. 'I don't know how to explain it, but God is sustaining me and I am doing great.'"

That supernatural peace continued to sustain Wilma until about two weeks after the funeral. She remembers that it felt like she had been in a bubble above the situation. But as she walked into the living room one particular day, she hit the floor and it felt as if the bubble burst. It was then that she sensed the Lord say, *It's time for you to pray now.*

In that moment, Wilma realized the power of the prayers of her friends and family that had lifted her above the situation when she couldn't stand alone. She learned through those many difficult years that trials in our lives can either be stumbling blocks or stepping-stones.

"As I think back over Cherree's life, I see how God carried me through those difficult years," Wilma reflects with a wisdom borne out of the fire of difficult experiences. "Since Cherree's death, rather than sorrow, I feel peace. The battle is over and actually we won because Cherree and Lee are both home now. We will see them again. I'm glad for the opportunity to share my story so that others can know that even when a storm is raging around you, God can give you a song."

Dear God, You know the trials I have been going through and You've seen every tear. I ask for Your grace to strengthen me and for the comfort of the Holy Spirit to wash away my pain. I trust that somehow You will turn this situation around for good, and I will give You all the glory. Amen.

THE BITTER DISTRESS

In my distress I called to the LORD;
I cried to my God for help.
From his temple he heard my voice;
my cry came before him, into his ears.

PSALM 18:6

Her husband asked why she was leaving.

"It's all right," she said.

As she saddled her donkey, the woman spoke in even, measured words to the servant who would accompany her: "Lead on: don't slow down for me unless I tell you."

The tone of her voice had caught his attention as he led the two beasts to the dirt road. In all the years he had worked for the family, he couldn't ever remember hearing such strength or urgency in her voice. He risked a glance at his master's wife as they started off at a brisk pace. Something was very wrong, although he knew not what. But he was certain it had something to do with the child.

It was early in the day when the young lad went out to meet his father who was supervising the workers in the field. Excitement radiated from his face as he dressed. He loved to be with his father when he surveyed the growing crops, but he especially loved harvest time. Each year he begged his mother for the opportunity to join the activity in the field. Finally, he was old enough to go by himself.

Now berating herself for letting the child go, the memory of that morning played again and again as she recalled watching her son's back as he ran to meet his father.

"Faster," she told the servant. "We must make haste," she reiterated before retreating again into her private and horrifying thoughts, remembering the still form of her son as the servant carried him back from the field.

"The master instructed me to bring him to you quickly," she recalled him saying. "He was fine one minute and the next he was screaming, clutching his head in pain," the servant offered, trying to explain the strange events that had taken place. Helplessly bowing his head, he backed out the door to return to the fields.

From that point, she held him, praying for a miracle, even as his breathing grew shallower and shallower. But he never regained consciousness.

As they continued the journey, the woman gave an involuntary shiver in spite of the afternoon heat. It was almost as though she could feel the cold from her son's lifeless form still clinging to her after she had laid his dead body on the bed of the prophet. The prophet...she knew in her heart that he was her only hope.

"Look, there is the Shunammite woman," Elisha spoke to his servant Gehazi, as he noticed the woman approaching them in the distance. "Run to meet her and ask her, 'Are you all right? Is your husband all right? Is your child all right?'"

As the woman approached Elisha, he realized the distress of her heart.

"Did I ask you for a son, my lord? Didn't I tell you, 'Don't raise my hopes'?" she spoke, remembering the joy in her heart as Elisha had interceded to God on her behalf for a child.

It had only been a few years before when she asked her husband to build the extra room for the respected prophet so that he would have a place to stay whenever he traveled to their region. The hospitality she had extended to Elisha had been without desire for compensation. Yet, God saw her deepest desire and rewarded her with the very thing she had long before given up as impossible—a son.

The woman knelt before the prophet—pleading, yet resolute, unwilling to return home without a miracle. This woman's deep love manifested into action as the Shunammite woman refused to accept the death of God's blessing, her son. Her love mixed with faith brought another blessing, the restoration of his life.[24]

[24] Story based upon 2 Kings 4:8–36.

LIFE LESSONS

1. (Agape) love never gives up. In the face of adversity, it rises to the occasion, choosing faith and hope.
2. Love produces action when necessary, silence when needed, and strength in the storm.
3. God's love produces miracles.

SECTION 9

Love Thy Neighbor

Never does the human soul appear
so strong as when it foregoes revenge
and dares to forgive an injury.

EDWIN HUBBEL CHAPIN

Bitter or Better[25]

Joyce Meyer

Get rid of all bitterness, rage, anger, harsh words, and slander, as well as all types of malicious behavior. Instead, be kind to each other, tenderhearted, forgiving one another, just as God through Christ has forgiven you.

EPHESIANS 4:31–32 NLT

I thank God that Jesus came to heal the brokenhearted and to comfort those who mourn. Isaiah 61:3 says He even wants to give us "beauty instead of ashes"—to take from us all the pain and tragedy of the past and give us His joy, healing, and restoration!

If you're like most people, you have probably dealt with hurtful situations in the past. Maybe you've been taken advantage of, abused, or lied to. Or perhaps you have been deceived, misunderstood, or cheated out of something. Many, if not most, of us have been in this painful place, and some of you may be there right now.

[25] Reprinted with permission. "Bitter or Better" by Joyce Meyer © 2004, Joyce Meyer Ministries, monthly ministry letter—August 2004. All rights reserved.

I know one thing for certain—God does not want us to harbor bitterness or live life weighed down by the pain of the past! You *can* be free, and today, I want to share some principles that will help you live free from bitterness, resentment, and unforgiveness.

Years ago, God spoke something to my heart that I will never forget. He said, "Joyce, you can either be *bitter* or *better*." He showed me that bitterness is like poison—it makes us unhappy, sour, and hard to get along with. However, through the grace of God, you and I can learn to take the things that Satan arranges to make us bitter and allow them to make us better!

I was sexually abused for many years during my childhood. At age eighteen, I was finally able to *physically* walk away from the situation, but by that time roots of bitterness and resentment were deeply embedded in me. After Dave and I got married, I began to take my frustration, anger, and bitterness out on him—I was trying to make him pay me back for something he didn't do!

The bitter roots were causing bitter fruit—I was mad, irritable, filled with self-pity, and unable to control my emotions. I tried and tried to change the way I was acting, but I didn't know how.

Thankfully, the Lord showed me what the problem was—I was trying to remove the "bad fruit," but I wasn't getting to the root. One by one, He showed me I was dealing with roots of abuse, shame, guilt, and rejection. He then led me to specific scriptures that, over time, brought healing to my wounded emotions. I discovered God's deep love for me and developed a healthy sense of my own worth and value. Once I began dealing with the roots, I was able to eliminate the fruit.

Anger that is not dealt with will eventually grow into roots of resentment and bitterness. *Now, I don't think we can keep ourselves totally free from feeling angry after we've been hurt, but the thing we can and must do is deal with the anger quickly and correctly.*

Ephesians 4:26 AMP says, "When angry, do not sin; do not ever let your wrath (your exasperation...) last until the sun goes down." In other words, God gives us a little space of time to get control over our emotions. He wants us to make the decision to forgive, lean on Him for His grace, and thank Him for victory throughout the process.

When we are tempted to get angry or bitter, we need to run to God in prayer the moment we begin to feel aggravation and frustration trying to come on. He will provide us with the power to keep ourselves calm when adversity arises. (See Ps. 94:13.)

It's also important for us to renew our minds with the Word. We need to look up every scripture we can find on things like forgiveness, maintaining peace, and walking in love. Then we need to read them over and over, allowing the Holy Spirit to transform our thinking and minister healing to our emotions. God will give us the grace to be able to do what the Word is saying—all we need to do is ask for it.

I encourage you to make a decision today to forgive those who have hurt you and then immediately lean on God for the grace to do it. When you choose to forgive, it will actually benefit you much more than it will ever benefit them!

When I look back at my life, I can truly say that God worked out for my good what the devil meant for harm. (See Gen. 50:20.) God has even used some of the most painful experiences from my past to help thousands of others gain freedom from similar circumstances.

God wants to do the same thing for you. He is a God of restoration, and He loves you unconditionally. Whatever you are going through today, or whatever you may have endured in the past, He is ready and willing to walk you through it and help you live a life free from bitterness, resentment, and unforgiveness.

Give God a chance to prove Himself faithful in your life today. It will be the best decision you have ever made.

Heavenly Father, You know everything I have been through in my life, and You understand better than anyone the pain and anger I've dealt with. I choose to forgive those who have hurt me, and I receive Your love to heal my wounded heart. Amen.

Betrayed!

Dorothy's Story

And when you stand praying, if you hold anything against anyone, forgive him, so that your Father in heaven may forgive you your sins.

Mark 11:25

Dorothy and her husband, Peter, had their own business, were active in church, and had three beautiful children. Everything was going well until a business reversal turned their world upside down. As a result, Dorothy went into a severe depression, which eventually brought her to the brink of suicide.

"I didn't want to go out or do anything. I felt betrayed and deeply hurt by this Christian businessman, and I blamed him for our problems. Ultimately, I felt God had failed us," Dorothy shares of the painful event that began a downward spiral of her emotional and mental well-being.

"I began having frequent migraine headaches. Pain pills eased the pain in my head, but not in my heart. Eventually I began to take an antidepressant as well," she shares.

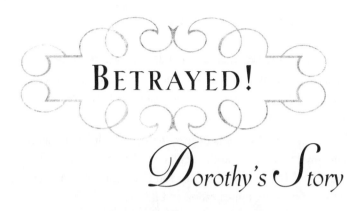

"Knowing I needed help, but almost against my will, my husband took me to a ladies' home Bible study. Since I didn't really want to be there, I kept my pain to myself, unwilling to let them reach out and pray for me.

"After weeks in this depressive state, I felt like I wanted to end my life. I waited until my children left for school and my husband left for his office. All I had to do was take an overdose of my prescription medication and it would all be over.

"As I was going to get the pills, the phone began to ring. On the line was a member of our church. He had never called before, but that day felt compelled to call and check on me. 'Dorothy, how are you?' he asked. 'Everything is just fine,' I lied, crying softly, knowing what I had been planning to do. But even with a well-meaning friend, I couldn't open my heart to share my need for prayer. The conversation ended quickly. But with this diversionary call, the overwhelming thoughts of suicide had been broken, however, the unforgiveness I harbored in my heart had not."

The Bible is clear regarding the necessity of forgiveness. According to Matthew 18:21–22, "Then Peter came to Jesus and asked, 'Lord, how many times shall I forgive my brother when he sins against me? Up to seven times?' Jesus answered, 'I tell you, not seven times, but seventy-seven times." That kind of forgiveness is impossible in our own strength. Thank God He gives us His strength as Dorothy would soon learn.

"You have to forgive," my husband Peter reminded me frequently. "I have," I always responded, thinking in my heart that this was the truth. But one day as we were going up the escalator to attend church, I saw the man I had accused of hurting us. "I hope he falls and breaks his neck," I whispered to my husband. Peter gave me a knowing smile as the truth dawned in my heart. I had not really forgiven him!

"In the midst of this struggle, our pastor began teaching on the necessity of forgiveness. *That's easy for you to say,* I thought to myself. *You've never been hurt like we have.*

"At that moment I heard the Lord speak to my heart, *Dorothy, you don't understand the hurt I experienced when I hung on the cross.*

"This time I began to ask God for what seemed impossible to me. I asked Him to help me forgive, but my newfound resolve was about to be tested," Dorothy continues sharing about her difficult experience.

"A few weeks later as we were sitting in church, our pastor asked us to turn and shake hands with the people around us. I turned and shook the hand of a lady behind me. It was the wife of the man I had come to despise! Yet somehow, I never saw her face. Next, I moved to shake her husband's hand. It was the moment of truth. Without a pause, I looked straight into his eyes and from the depths of my heart said to him, 'God bless you.'

"As the words left my mouth, it was as if honey was poured over my head and down to my feet. I let go of his hand and turning to Peter whispered, 'The bitterness is completely gone.' As I had spoken a blessing over this man, it had unlocked the hurt from my heart, setting me completely free," Dorothy shared with a tone of voice that reveals the depth of her release.

Now for the past sixteen years, Dorothy has led the very Bible study that her husband took her to eighteen years ago in her moment of need. During that time, almost two thousand ladies have attended, with six members from the original group still taking part today.

"The women who attend come from all walks of life and various churches," Dorothy continues. Many have been wounded by broken marriages or have been betrayed by friends. Not everyone is hurting in the same way, but all of us have challenges we face.

"Because of my own painful experience, I am able to reach out to others in their time of need. I have learned that we always have a choice. We can either become bitter or become better. I never wanted to go through the pain we experienced, but this very pain has enabled me to help others and find my own purpose in life.

"I have never enjoyed life more than I do today," she finishes.

Dorothy's joy for living was completely restored, in spite of the act of betrayal, once she decided to extend the hand of forgiveness.

Dear Lord, I choose to forgive and release the pain and hurts of my past. Set me free from the bondage of an unforgiving heart to see and love others as You do. Amen.

But God, I Don't Want to Love Them

If it is possible, as far as it depends on you,
live at peace with everyone.

Romans 12:18

Some things are just easier to love and appreciate than others. Take chocolate for example or warm fuzzy kittens, a beautiful sunset or a crisp October sky. Some things hold an almost universal appeal, although it might be difficult to explain why.

On the other hand, there are things that can repel us just as strongly. Unfortunately, that sometimes includes people.

It's easy to love people who agree with us, think like we do, and love us. That's a given. But the command to "love thy neighbor" comes without conditions. No one ever said it was going to be easy...but it is mandatory.

My husband, Kevin, and I first met "Dave and Kelly" when we were placed together on an overseas ministry outreach team, meaning that we would work closely with them for the next six years. We shared a zeal to communicate the love of Christ to those who had never heard. Unfortunately, that was about the only thing we had in common.

This couple was about as loveable and cuddly as a porcupine poised for attack. But then again, they probably felt the same about us. It might not have been a problem had we not been assigned lodging on the same floor of an apartment complex consisting of only three apartments—theirs, ours, and another couple's—making frequent contact unavoidable. Not to mention that after a season, Kevin and I were put into a leadership capacity over the ministry outreach team. This new development seemed to add insult to injury for Dave and Kelly, who were approximately ten years our senior. From that point on, the relationship made a speedy descent.

"Honey, it's impossible," I sighed in frustration on more than one occasion as Kevin and I discussed the situation. "It doesn't matter what I say, Kelly disagrees with me. It's like she's just looking for a fight."

"It can't be that bad," my husband—the perpetual peacemaker—consoled.

But it was.

Not long after, as our team went on a short-term outreach to a different area, I decided to test my theory. Overhearing Kelly's conversation with another teammate, I learned of her interest in a specific type of music. She said she felt a sense of comfort and nostalgia each time she heard specific songs.

Later in the day as Kelly and I found ourselves seated across from each other, I made another stab at friendship.

Keep it even, I reminded myself mentally, walking on eggshells as I worked at making acceptable conversation. A few minutes of pleasantries were exchanged before I brought the conversation around to music. Having overheard Kelly's preference in that area, I felt I was finally in safe waters.

Turning the comment that I had overheard into a question, I asked, "Don't you sometimes miss the music we grew up with?"

Already anticipating her answer, I was shocked when Kelly leveled her gaze at me and took aim. "No, I have completely adjusted to our new ministry environment and don't really miss anything. Besides, music isn't what is supposed to bring us comfort in the first place."

Another conversation derailed.

No, it really didn't seem to matter what Kevin or I said to this couple as they repeatedly let us know their disdain for us. Living in peace with them seemed a fleeting hope.

We tried various forms of reconciliation. We invited them over for dinner. I made soup for them when they were ill. We even helped them replace their bikes when they were stolen—not once, but twice. But nothing we did seemed to smooth the turbulent waters between us.

From time to time, I even learned of comments they had made about us to others in the form of "prayer requests." These often became ugly rumors that circulated, undermining the effectiveness of our leadership with the group.

In all fairness, Kevin and I were far from perfect. Young in our leadership skills, we made numerous mistakes with the team as a whole, not to mention our dealings with Dave and Kelly. I certainly had to make frequent attitude adjustments and learn to keep my mouth shut. There were many times when I wanted to retaliate against their constant stealthy attacks, to defend myself before my attackers, but I knew this would only prolong the war. Our attempts to talk with them about areas of disagreement were simply ignored.

Returning to our apartment one afternoon, I found a note taped to the door. Unlocking the door and placing my packages on the table, I began to read the letter. I slowly sat down, stunned.

In the note, Dave and Kelly had made a list of grievances against us ranging in degrees from how we ministered and how we dressed to conversations we had engaged in. The letter was not just one page, but three. But the most difficult thing as I read through the numbered offenses was that the majority were based on situations in which neither Dave nor Kelly had been present. The only way they could have heard about the situations was through word of mouth. There was little truth in any of their stinging accusations.

My first reaction was a swelling anger as I felt heat flood my face. *How dare they piously accuse us of things they have no real facts about!* I thought. Not to mention that they were not even willing to address us with their frustrations face-to-face in a biblical manner.

Fortunately, within moments I sensed the Holy Spirit speak to my heart. *Forgive.*

I knew it had to be God's prompting because that was about the last thing in my heart at that particular moment. Yet as I took a deep breath, I knew it was right. This had to stop somewhere.

I prayed for several minutes before taking pen and paper to respond to each and every grievance Dave and Kelly had listed. Instead of defending ourselves, I simply apologized to them, slowly working my way through the pages, addressing each attack with an apology and sometimes sharing a few of the details they may not have heard about. After completing the note, I reread it to make sure it was free of any animosity or sound of defensiveness. In that moment I understood that it really didn't matter what Dave and Kelly thought about us as long as Kevin and I were able to walk in love and forgiveness... regardless of their response. I folded the letter and put it into an envelope, then walked across the hall to their apartment and taped my response to their door.

And I prayed.

When Kevin returned that afternoon, I shared with him what had transpired regarding the letter, the accusations, and my response. His anger initially flared the same as mine had, but I watched as almost immediately that same supernatural peace flooded over him as well. We chose to let it go.

The next day after lunch there was a knock at the door. I was more than surprised to see Kelly standing at our door with the letter in her hand. "I am so sorry," she began, embarrassment evident on her face. "We obviously didn't have all the facts. Will you please forgive us?"

There were many tears that day as we joined together in prayer, choosing to work together on the difficult relationship. And while I can't say that the relationship was always perfect after that day, I can say that His love and forgiveness were.

Dear God, Your ways are truly higher than ours and I can only walk in them by Your grace. When I am hurt by others, help me to be quick to forgive and not allow bitterness to take root in my heart. Help me to make the first move toward reconciliation so that I can be a peacemaker. Amen.

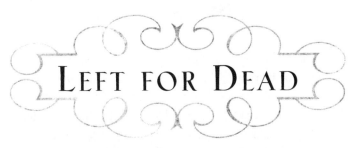

LEFT FOR DEAD

But he wanted to justify himself, so he asked Jesus, "And who is my neighbor?"

LUKE 10:29

The man had heard the warnings that were circulating across the city; however, he paid little attention to gossip or rumors and had only listened halfheartedly to this latest buzz.

"So what is this I hear about the road being unsafe to travel on alone?" he asked the merchant as he purchased the needed supplies for his trip. Always welcoming a listening ear, the merchant willingly rattled off the harrowing details he had heard in recent weeks.

The businessman shook his head in disbelief. He had traveled the route hundreds of times since childhood and had never had a moment's concern. It was true enough, he admitted, that theft had gradually increased as times had grown difficult, but murder? He couldn't believe it. He wouldn't believe it. This was his home. He was born and raised in the city and had raised his own children there as well.

It is a good place, indeed a safe place, he reassured himself.

He loaded his materials on the back of the donkey in preparation for the journey to the town where he had business. If he got an early start, he could most likely arrive before nightfall, eliminating any need for concern. He hurried to finish packing, carefully placing the silver coins in a small pouch, which he tucked into the hidden pocket of his leather bag. The days had grown cooler with the approach of autumn. The trip would be pleasant enough, and he anticipated a lucrative conclusion to the business transaction that awaited.

The road was deserted for the most part, although on two occasions the man passed other travelers, both in pairs, going the opposite direction. He waved as they passed, noting the increased rate of his heart. Those stories had had an effect after all. Taking a deep breath, he continued on, keeping an eye on the position of the sun. He should make it in plenty of time.

As the sun began to disappear and the low light of dusk began to settle, the man picked up his pace. He was just a few miles from his destination, which he knew was just around the last bend. As he shifted his shoulder bag to the other side, he heard a noise; but by the time he saw their shadows, it was too late.

Alone, he didn't stand a chance. As the robbers beat and bruised his body, he wondered fleetingly what death would be like, pain racking his being. Finally, it was more than his body could stand, and he fell unconscious, oblivious to their merciless onslaught.

With one last kick, the robbers rolled his limp body into the ditch on the side of the road. After stripping him of his clothes and grabbing the leather pouch, they started off. "He won't be needing these anymore," the calloused robber laughed to his compatriot.

It was cold. The man unconsciously shivered, sending throbbing pain to every part of his body as he drifted back into consciousness. Vividly he recalled the beating from the previous night and noted the early rays of sunlight in the eastern sky. His mouth was dry. As the pain from his injuries penetrated his consciousness, he willingly allowed himself to sink back into oblivion.

Not long after a priest happened on the road. As he came near the bloodied businessman, he cautiously looked behind him. Noting the absence of fellow travelers, he crossed to the opposite side of the road and continued on the path without a second look at the man in need.

Several hours later, a Levite, one selected to work in the temple, passed along the same road. Like the priest, he, too, noticed the naked, wounded man and crossed to the opposite side without slowing his pace.

If I stop, the man reasoned to himself, *I'll never make it to the city by nightfall. Besides, I've been hearing how dangerous this road can be...*

Finally, a Samaritan traveling down the road spotted the wounded man and walked directly to him. *At least he is breathing,* he thought as he gently rolled the man over and began to bandage the most obvious wounds. Once finished, he placed the victim on his own donkey and led him into town to the local inn. Once he secured lodging, he labored to clean the deep cuts and wash away the crusted blood. The man groaned at the applied pressure, but never opened his eyes.

The next morning the Samaritan quietly shut the door as he left the room of the injured man. Handing the innkeeper two silver coins he directed, "Look after him. When I return, I will reimburse you for any extra expense he requires."

The innkeeper stared at the man and stuttered in disbelief. "Didn't you realize he was a Jew? Why would you help him? He certainly would not have done the same for you."

The Samaritan only smiled as he walked out of the inn.[26]

Life Lessons

1. The story of the Good Samaritan has never been more relevant than today as prejudices abound between Arab and Jew, black and white, conservative and liberal. Only by "loving thy neighbor as thyself" can God heal the wounds of the past and present and bring lasting peace.
2. Can you relate to the priest and Levite who saw their fellow man in need, yet refused to help? Were they too busy? Perhaps they considered it beneath their dignity. Or were they afraid for their own safety? Search your own

[26] Story based upon Luke 10:30–37.

heart and look around. There are hurting people every-where in need of assistance. The question we must always ask ourselves is, "What if it were me?"

3. What does it mean to "love thy neighbor as thyself"? The erroneous thought that only the man next door is our neighbor must give way to the reality that our neighbor is in fact every person who crosses our path.

Agape Love

There is nothing you can do to
make God love you more!
There is nothing you can do to
make God love you less!
His love is unconditional,
impartial, everlasting,
infinite, perfect! God is love!

AUTHOR UNKNOWN

SECTION 10

Transforming Love

In the natural world it is impossible to be made all over again, but in the spiritual world it is exactly what Jesus Christ makes possible.

Oswald Chambers

CHANGED AND IT SHOWS

Libby Hodges

PREVIOUSLY OF JUMP 5

AS TOLD TO KAREN HARDIN

Don't let anyone look down on you because you are young, but set an example for the believers in speech, in life, in love, in faith and in purity.

1 TIMOTHY 4:12

It's often difficult for teens to be around people their own age. Peer pressure and temptation start at a much younger age than it has in previous generations. In my own life, there was a time when even though I was a Christian, I doubt that anyone could tell it by looking at me.

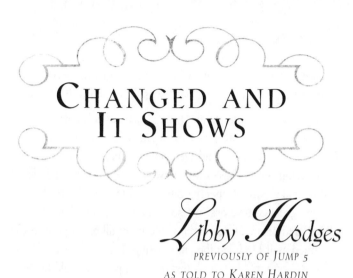

Then, during the summer before I went into the sixth grade, I attended a church camp in Tennessee. I began to realize that although I had made a decision for Christ when I was six or seven, there was little outward evidence of that decision. It wasn't that I was a bad kid, but I wasn't living my life for God.

But a week at this camp changed my outlook permanently. Way out in the boonies, staying in rustic log cabins, we had plenty of time to sit around the campfire and share with each other. Being out in the open and away from the typical daily routine had a way of opening our hearts to God. With the help of some great counselors, we spent hours playing, laughing, talking, and crying. One night as we were all crying out to God, it seemed as if He filled the entire camp. He was there and we knew it. You wouldn't think that a young person could have such a serious encounter with God, but it was real and it changed my life.

Being a Christian takes a decision. And it requires a further decision to share Christ with those around us, but these are decisions I have made. As a teen, I now realize that it's not about being cool or trying to change my personality or image to get a guy or group of girls to like me. It just isn't worth it. Staying true to oneself and to God are the most important things a person can do. Whatever you want to be in life, you can be if you will dare to go after your dreams and stand against the temptation to be someone you aren't. God made you who you are, and He made you just right.

LIBBY HODGES, seventeen, has from the age of five followed her singer/actress mother's lead, embarking on a career in entertainment. Now entering a new season, Libby has said good-bye to her successful singing partners, Jump 5. She plans to take a missions trip with Youth with a Mission (YWAM) before entering college. Libby resides with her parents, older brother, and younger sister in Nashville, Tennessee.

Dear God, thank You for sending Jesus to give me new life. I choose to live for You today and pray that You will help me to live in such a way that others will be drawn to You. Continue Your transforming work in me so that I can be all You've designed for me to be. Amen.

Finding Love in a Faraway Land

Nicole's Story

God is working in you to help you want to do and be able to do what pleases him.

Philippians 2:13 NCV

"I was only five years old when my family lived in Japan where my father was stationed with the CIA. One day, sitting on a grassy knoll overlooking the Sea of China near our home, I had a vision of myself as an adult with my arms around almond-eyed people, telling them about Jesus. I didn't know it at the time, but I was looking in the direction of my future. That was almost forty-five years ago," Nicole begins as she shares of a most remarkable decision that would take her to a remarkable land.

Near Nicole's home in Japan was a group of Catholic missionaries. They wore long sparkling white habits in sharp contrast to the shabby and drab outfits of the Japanese people after World War II. After a typhoon swept through the area, Nicole remembers seeing these nuns, accompanied by a man who looked to her like Jesus, carrying people on stretchers to receive medical attention. Their loving actions made an indelible impression on the young girl's heart.

A few years later, Nicole's family relocated back to America. The fast-paced American culture quickly wiped away memories of her early years in Asia as she completed her education and started down her career path. Eventually, she opened her own business, but experienced a roller coaster of both success and financial hardships.

"At twenty-seven, overwhelmed by the constant financial pressures and weight of running the business, I began visiting churches near home, hungering for more meaning in life," Nicole candidly shares. "Three years later, I had an amazing salvation experience, giving my heart to the Lord. It was a decision that not only changed my life, but would change my location as well."

A couple of years later, after learning of China's great need for the Gospel, Nicole found herself moving to China where she worked first as an English teacher in a medical academy. Her students were young doctors and nurses. Their childlike innocence and desire to help others touched her heart.

"Since China is a communist country, I was forbidden to openly share the Gospel. Yet time and time again, our classroom discussions would drift toward religion," Nicole remembers.

"Each time they did, the colonel assigned to monitor the class and our conversation would stand up and walk out of the room, allowing the discussion to continue," she says in amazement.

The longer Nicole remained in Asia, the more she had a heart to reach the lost and hurting around her, eventually establishing a medical work to bring assistance and training to rural areas. Today, Nicole has established both a hospital and an orphanage for special-needs children. In addition, she continues to bring in numerous medical professionals from around the world to provide free short-term medical clinics to this needy land.

"God has also blessed me with a beautiful daughter," Nicole continues. "Missy was abandoned in a box in front of a train station when she was two years old. Born with spina bifida and two clubfeet, her parents had been unable to provide the medical assistance she needed. When she was brought to me, she was sick and weak, but possessed such a sweet spirit that I was immediately drawn to her," Nicole shares. "After several surgeries, Missy's physical limitations have been greatly reduced. One of my greatest joys was in finally completing the lengthy adoption process, legally confirming what was already true in our hearts. We are now 'a family.'

"Sometimes I think back to that five-year-old little girl in Japan, looking across the Sea of China," Nicole concludes. "God knew then the direction my life would take, surrounding me with an amazing people from a faraway land."

Dear God, I know You have a divine plan for my life, and I ask You to give me a love for that work and lead me to it. Whatever "career" You have for me, I promise to be faithful in pursuing it. Nothing that has happened in my life has been unforeseen by You, and I ask You to help me to continue to grow and to use it all for Your glory. Amen.

The Great Escape

Darla's Story

I do not understand what I do. For what I want to do I do not do, but what I hate I do.

Romans 7:15

"Half of my body was engulfed in the flames that wrapped themselves around my legs like fingers. They kept grabbing me, pulling me further and further down while the rest of me was in a place of incredible light and beauty. Even in this strange semi-conscious state, I could feel the battle of the light pulling me upward. That was where I was supposed to be. I struggled to free my lower body, but the flames kept pulling me back...."

Darla woke up in a sweat, trying to shake the recurring images from her mind. She knew this dream well. It represented the war for her soul that was constantly tugging at her heart. She wanted and prayed for change. She didn't want to do the wrong things, yet she did them over and over again.

"My parents divorced as I was entering into the preadolescent years," Darla shares, reflecting back to the catalyst that, she believes, started her on a destructive path. "Looking for an escape from the confusion and pain, I became something of a loner. When I did hang with friends, it was a tough crowd. It didn't take long to realize that I enjoyed the fast-paced adventure and thrill of the new elements to which they introduced me. By the time I was fourteen, I was smoking pot and drinking on a regular basis. Those two goodies eventually escalated into harder drugs. In an attempt to rein my life back under control, I transferred to a Christian school during my senior year of high school. But even though I had 'cleaned up' my life, I still didn't seem to fit in. My difficulty in making friends only increased my feelings of rejection until I returned to my previous habits of drinking and drugs."

After high school graduation, Darla became a bartender. The money was great, but the lifestyle and the people she met through this job soon took her even deeper into the fast-moving world of drugs. In a relatively short time, she began not only using cocaine, but dealing it and other drugs as well. Always looking for a new adventure, she decided on a whim to move to South Padre Island with whatever would fit into her car and enough cocaine to get her there. She easily landed another bartending job and soon made new friends to party with. Darla's destructive habits had just reached a new level.

One night Darla and a friend were packaging up eight balls—large amounts of cocaine that they were splitting up for resale. It was between 2:00 and 3:00 A.M. when the phone rang. Her mother was on the other end.

"Darla, are you okay? The Lord woke me up, and I felt that I should call and check on you."

Darla looked at the cocaine spread across her table, "Sure Mom, I'm doing great," she replied, cutting the conversation short.

"No matter what I did or how bad things got, my mother was undeterred and continued to walk the floor at night praying for God's mercy and protection over my life," Darla remembers. "It was a protection I desperately needed as I continued my self-destructive path, which eventually included holding forty thousand dollars for an arms sale and a few stints in jail. I know I'm alive today largely because of her unrelenting prayers. I couldn't escape the Lord."

One day while still living on South Padre Island, Darla met "Scott." He was involved in the same lifestyle of drugs and parties. It was a comfortable relationship, and not long after, they decided to move in together to split the rent. About a year later, she discovered she was pregnant.

"Pregnancy added a great responsibility to my life," Darla states reflecting back to that time more than fifteen years ago. "Scott and I married and I immediately stopped using hard drugs, concerned of the effect they might have on my unborn child. About the same time, my brother and his wife called to offer me a job as a cartographer—a person who makes maps—in his graphic arts design company. Knowing I needed to make a new start, I wanted to accept his offer, but Scott was opposed to the move. Eventually I accepted the job and moved on ahead, not knowing if Scott would join me or not," Darla explains.

Eventually Scott did follow almost four months later.

"I've had people tell me that you can't walk away from heavy drugs such as cocaine without going through a drug rehabilitation program," Darla explains. "But I can honestly say that with every single drug I used, something finally rose up within me and I just walked away. Concern for my baby's health kept me straight, no problem," she admits.

Darla and Scott were finally getting their lives on track and it felt good. They had a beautiful, healthy baby boy, good jobs and were essentially drug free. That is, until Darla stopped nursing the baby. Once the mental barrier she had erected to protect the life of her baby was no longer needed, she and Scott eventually drifted back into their previous lifestyle of drug use. They found willing participants in their next-door neighbors as nightly parties became the norm, and the downhill slide started all over again.

Then the old dream began to recur as Darla prayed night after night for God to change her.

"I had always known God had a plan for my life," Darla states. "I hoped He would somehow pluck me out of that lifestyle. But the change wasn't that simple."

The more Darla tried to pull away from the grip of drugs on her life, the more her husband moved in deeper. Eventually they divorced when their son, Devon, was only three. Hoping to be free of the control of drugs, she soon found herself controlled in other ways.

"Not long after my divorce, I began hanging out with an old friend whom I eventually married. Although no drugs were involved, Ritchie was imprisoned in a different way. He would experience panic attacks that would paralyze him from normal activity, leaving him unwilling to leave the house and unable to sleep at night.

"During these bouts, he only listened to heavy metal rock music, walking through the house with his shoulders hunched over in a world of his own. He couldn't work since he refused to leave the house, but was also unwilling for me to leave during his bizarre attacks. Without a regular paycheck, we fell behind on our bills until the bank threatened to take our house. To make matters worse, I was now pregnant," Darla says.

At that point, Ritchie became abusive and even more erratic in his behavior. Finally, Darla had had enough and told Ritchie to get out. The marriage ended not long after, leaving her with $7500 in debt, a lawsuit, and not a dollar in her pocket. Finally, she was ready to turn her life back over to God, but what a mess.

"Now thirty-two years old, I was twice divorced with two small children, a jail record, and a history of drug use. It was then that I turned to God to be my husband and provider. And my family was right there to see me through this difficult time, helping me get back on my feet," Darla shares.

"I knew from a young age that I was called to the ministry, but it was difficult to see how God could ever use me. Even in the midst of doing drugs and smoking marijuana, I could not escape the reality of God's call on my life. Yet I wondered how God could ever use someone so unworthy of His love."

But He did. All Darla had at the time was a computer and the abilities God had given her. But that was enough and miracles began to happen.

Darla is now forty-one years old and married to Bill, a wonderful Christian man. He is a father to her two older children—Devon, 15; and Sierra, 9—and God has blessed them with another child, Hunter, age 5. Darla is a self-taught graphic designer, marketing consultant and owner of Holmes Consulting, and founder of Simply Being You Studios. The purpose of the latter is to teach young women etiquette, as well as conversational skills, confidence, and respect. Ultimately, she desires to start an inner-city teen center to minister to hurting and heartbroken youth.

"I want to reach out to the ones who don't feel like they belong. I want to let them know that God loves them, accepts them, and that He created them for a reason. I want to give them a passion for life."

Dear God, give me strength to choose Your ways and to say no to the things of this world, which threaten to take me down. Forgive me for the mistakes I've made and help get me back on track. Thank You for Your transforming love. Amen.

For more information about Simply Being You Studios, contact DARLA HOLMES at (918) 834-2107 or e-mail: darla.holmes@cox.net.

The Man in the Tombs

But because of his great love for us, God, who is rich in mercy, made us alive with Christ even when we were dead in transgressions—it is by grace you have been saved.

Ephesians 2:4–5

Kill them!

Return tonight once it is dark and give them their due for the way they have treated you.

Do it! It is your destiny...

The voices. Hundreds of them filled his mind, controlling his actions, his thoughts, his very life. At times the villagers had bound him hands and feet, but to no avail. His strength was far beyond that of any natural man—because that which possessed him was anything but natural.

Spiritually dead, he made his home among the dead, in the tombs outside the city where the voices that controlled his mind seemed to resonate back and forth against the caves. It never stopped.

Agitated, he watched as the boat pulled ashore. His head was again filled with the voices, which all seemed to be speaking at once as they sensed the Power drawing near. Threatened, the evil spirit moved his pawn into action.

While Jesus was still a far distance away, the man ran toward Him, his eyes as wild as his matted hair. Throwing himself down in front of Him, he screamed at the top of his lungs.

"What do you want with me, Jesus, Son of the Most High God?"

Sensing the impending doom, the spirit cried out to negotiate safe passage into another vessel. "Don't torture me!" it cried.

"What is your name?" Jesus commanded with authority.

"My name is Legion," he replied, "for we are many."

Able to see past the hideous creature the man had become, Jesus looked at him with compassion, seeing the man he was called to be. By His words, He commanded the man to be set free.

"Come out!" Jesus demanded.

As the evil spirit departed, the man's mind immediately returned to normal. He was free at last from the voices. The spirit, which had possessed him, was completely gone. The man's eyes no longer mirrored the evil reflection. In fear and reverence, he remained prostrate before the Lord.

"Let me go with you," he begged Jesus with overflowing gratitude.

Jesus looked on him with the Father's love and shook His head. "No, instead go tell your family all that the Lord has done for you."[27]

Life Lessons

1. Agape love, the love of the Father, transforms us. It breaks through the sin and evil resident within to bring us back to that which He has called us to be—His child.
2. Compassion. It is one of the notable ingredients of the Father's love that distinguishes it above all else. In spite of what we have done, His compassion allows us the opportunity to be drawn back to Him.
3. This transforming love not only sets free, but it also deposits a lasting joy and peace as it clears away the confusion of the world. It is available to all.

[27] Story based upon Mark 5:1–20.

SECTION 11

A Father's Love

Be absolutely certain that our Lord loves you,
devotedly and individually,
loves you just as you are....
Accustom yourself to the wonderful
thought that God loves you with a
tenderness, a generosity, and an intimacy
that surpasses all your dreams.

ABBE HENRI DE TOURVILLE

A Father to the Fatherless

Lesley Moore

of Jump 5

as told to Karen Hardin

I will instruct you and teach you in the way you should go;
I will counsel you and watch over you.

Psalm 32:8

I was just three years old when my dad died. I was so young that I hardly remember him at all. My mom has told me that he served in the army during the Vietnam War before they met. During his time in the service, he was shot in the leg and shoulder. Doctors told him he would never walk again. But they didn't know my dad. After months in the hospital, therapy, and leg braces, he not only walked, but played several sports such as golf, tennis, and softball!

It was more than fifteen years after the war that my dad was diagnosed with a rare form of cancer, and we believe it was caused by exposure to the deadly herbicide Agent Orange, used by the enemy during the war. After undergoing many kinds of treatments and enduring long hospitalizations, they finally tried a multiple-organ transplant, replacing his liver, pancreas, stomach, and part of his intestines. It was a risky and uncommon procedure. Although he made it through surgery, the symptoms continued until the cancer completely overtook his body, eventually taking his life.

Yes, this has been an incredible loss, but I don't consider myself to be a statistic. In fact, I don't feel I've missed all that much by not having my dad around. I believe the reason is that my grandfather and my uncle have been such great role models for me for as long as I can remember. Long ago when my mother would be at the hospital taking care of my father, my grandparents took care of me. Some of my earliest memories are of those times I had with them. My grandfather was a very dedicated man and faithfully took me to church with him, instilling Christian values in me when I was a very little girl.

Sure, there have been challenges, but my mother has worked hard to make sure I have had the same opportunities as other kids. Somehow she has found the time and resources to provide me with singing lessons, dance lessons, or any other thing I have wanted to be involved in. Whatever void I have experienced in life, my family and faith in God have helped to fill it.

God has truly been a Father to me while also providing me with a family who has taught me the real meaning of love.

Dear God, thank You for being a Father to me and for filling up the empty places created by life's circumstances. Thank You for bringing godly people and friends along my path to help me along the way and to remind me that I am not alone. Amen.

LESLEY MOORE, eighteen and always energetic, is never at a loss for words. Like her friends in Jump 5, Lesley began entertaining at a very young age. She has appeared in many commercials and music videos and now tours with Jump 5. She resides in Nashville, Tennessee, with her mother.

It Wasn't My Alarm Clock

Ruthie's Story

[Jesus said], "If you, then, though you are evil,
know how to give good gifts to your children,
how much more will your Father in heaven
give good gifts to those who ask Him!"

MATTHEW 7:11

It was October 22, 1991, a night Ruthie and her family will forever remember as a night of miracles. Ruthie was eleven years old, the second of four kids. She and her family were all sound asleep, her mom having gone to bed last around 12:30 A.M. Just an hour and a half later, the incessant sound awoke her father. He waited patiently at first and then with growing annoyance for the penetrating buzzer to cease.

Ruthie, turn off the alarm, he thought as he climbed out of bed and stumbled to stand. Resigning himself to the fact that he was going to have to turn the alarm off himself, he squinted to clear his vision and his mind. The dim light from the night-light in the hallway cast a hazy glow in the smoke as realization finally hit. The noise wasn't Ruthie's alarm clock. It was the fire alarm!

"'Fire! Fire! There's a fire! Get out!' my father screamed repeatedly. 'Get out!' The house was ablaze," Ruthie shares, painting a vivid image of that night almost fifteen years ago. "Mom woke at the sound of Dad's screams and together they worked to rouse my sister, two brothers, and me. Hands outstretched to compensate for the vision marred from the smoke, Dad stumbled, hurrying his way·through the dense cloud of smoke. Finally, he found his way to the front door. His hand sizzled as he grabbed the burning metal of the doorknob. But it wouldn't budge. The force of the fire, sucking for the outside air, created a vacuum, firmly holding the door in place, preventing our escape. Before his eyes the latch began to melt over the door so intense was the heat at that moment," she recounts.

"We had only moments to get out."

With no alternative escape available, Ruthie's dad pounded and pulled at the door, finally winning the desperate tug of war. Her mom, sister, and brother ran out the opening as her dad followed. What they didn't realize was that Ruthie and her youngest brother were still inside.

"Confused and alone in the smoky darkness, I heard Mom outside yelling, 'Billy Joe, Ruthie and Paul are still in there!'

"With no thought for his own safety, my dad raced back into the inferno, the heavy smoke searing his lungs as he labored for air," Ruthie recounts. "He began waving his arm back and forth in front of him, frantically searching for us. Relief flooded over me as I felt his hand brush the top of my head."

As he grabbed Ruthie's hair and pulled her to safety, the two dashed for the front door.

Leaving her on the lawn, he immediately raced back to the house for Paul. With blistered hands, he grasped the hot metal knob once again to reenter what had been their home. His eyes and lungs burned as he groped again in the smoky mass for his six-year-old son. The smoke increased, choking out what little air remained. Bending low to the ground, once again he began swinging his arm in a back-and-forth motion down the dark hall, racing against the growing danger. At the end of the hall, his hands found Paul. Grabbing him in his arms, he raced back to the entryway and out the door, just as the front window exploded.

Now safely on the front lawn, the family huddled together in the cool night air, a striking contrast to the flames engulfing their home and reaching for the sky.

"I'll never forget that night and the depth of my father's love," Ruthie explains with emotion. "Those horrifying moments alone in the fiery house burned an indelible memory in my heart. For without a moment's hesitation for his own safety, my father ran back to save us. That is the true reflection of a father's love. It is a mirror of the depth of our Heavenly Father's love.

"My dad was hospitalized for smoke inhalation and burns to his hands and eyes, all which healed over time. The house was destroyed. But everything that was lost was nothing compared to being alive as a family. We were all safe and secure, both physically and in the amazing love of our dad who taught me the true meaning of a father's love."

Father God, thank You for Your amazing and boundless love for me. Thank You that because of that love, You never sleep or slumber but are constantly watching over me, commissioning Your angels to guard and protect me, keeping me safe from harm. I'm thankful that You are my Father and I am Your child. Amen.

Ruthie Daugherty Sanders and her husband, Adam, are youth ministers at Victory Christian Center in Tulsa, Oklahoma.

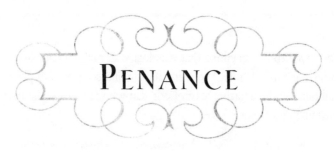

PENANCE

For it is by grace you have been saved, through faith— and this not from yourselves, it is the gift of God— not by works, so that no one can boast.

EPHESIANS 2:8–9

The dark-skinned Costa Rican man walked over to the foreigner who had stooped to pick up his burdensome load. With questioning eyes, he watched as the medium-built American positioned the enormous weight upon one shoulder. With a hesitant voice, he asked, "Can I carry it for you?" The load the man carried was a cross.

Since 1985, Keith Wheeler has traveled to 146 countries and seven continents carrying a twelve foot, ninety pound cross. Its two weather-beaten timbers are attached to a small wheel at its base to enable Wheeler to carry the cross into even the most remote regions of the world including Antarctica, Iran, Iraq, China, and more. He goes not as a tourist or an activist, but as a pilgrim with a message. On this particular journey, Keith had started in Panama and was slowing winding his way to Mexico when he stopped in this small Costa Rican village to talk with its occupants.

A group of approximately forty men, women, and children surrounded him as he spoke a message of freedom from sin and the sacrifice of the cross. Once he finished he turned to pick up the cross to continue his journey. As he bent down, an older man, struck with the weight of his own sin, requested permission to carry the cross in Keith's place. Before he positioned the beam across his own bony shoulder, he bent down to roll up his pant legs. Next, he removed his shoes, exposing his bare feet. As they walked, the old man made a winding path, purposely stepping on every jagged rock, briar, and piece of broken glass that littered their path. The weight of the cross and the wounds on his now bloodied feet, a penance for the sin in his life—a weight much heavier than the physical cross he now carried.

"This is not about penance. You don't have to carry the cross," Keith explained. "Jesus already did it for you. You don't have to shed your blood. He already did that for you. You don't have to suffer. Jesus already suffered for you." Over the next seven miles, the two journeyed together as Keith continued to share of the mighty work that transpired on the cross more than two thousand years ago.

"You don't understand," the man stated, unable to look Wheeler in the eyes. "I am a bad man and have done many bad things." He grimaced, but uttered no sound as he stepped on the shard of glass in front of him, the weight of the cross pushing his foot full force on the object. Sweat poured down the man's face as he continued on, determination etched on his weathered face.

Over and over, Wheeler slowly repeated, "You can never do anything in yourself that will remove the weight of sin, but Jesus has already paid the price on the cross. All you have to do is accept Him and your sins will be gone, completely forgiven.

"All you have to do is welcome Him into your life," Keith exhorted, watching as the blood trickled down the legs of the man next to him. "You only have to receive Him."

As they came to the crest of a steep hill, suddenly the realization of Wheeler's words found their mark in the man's heart as a new light shone from his eyes. Slowly removing the cross from his shoulder, he handed it back to Keith, at the same time releasing the burden of sin he had shouldered for so many years.

"You mean I didn't have to carry this cross? You mean, I'm free?"

As Keith nodded, the man jumped in the air, literally clicked his heels together, and let out a mighty yell, "I'M FREE! I'M FREE!" With that he turned and began racing back down the mountain toward his home, shouting as he went. "I'm *free!*"

At last he really was.

Oh God, You are so good! Thank You for Jesus who willingly bore my sin and shame. The enormity of that sacrifice is more than I can fully comprehend, yet I embrace it so that I can walk in freedom—free to love You, to serve You, and to fulfill the destiny You've planned for me. Amen.

For more information on the ministry of KEITH WHEELER, write: P. O. Box 471035, Tulsa, OK 74147, USA. Or e-mail: keith@kw.org.

The Father's Heart[28]

Richard Exley

[Jesus said], "For God so loved the world that he gave his one and only Son, that whoever believes in him shall not perish but have eternal life."

JOHN 3:16

An eternity past, before I laid the foundations of the world, I embraced this fateful day. When the creation of man was just a distant thought, and his fall an unrealized tragedy, I committed Myself to redemption's plan. Still, now that the time has come, I find I am grievously pained at what must be done.

My heart is torn as Jesus pleads with Me, "Abba, Father," He says, "everything is possible for You. Take this cup from Me."

It is all I can do not to snatch that deadly cup from His trembling hands and hurl its toxic dregs into outer darkness. But

---

[28] Reprinted with permission. *Witness the Passion* by Richard Exley © 2004. Published by White Stone Books, Lakeland, Florida.

what would that accomplish, beyond a momentary reprieve? In truth, it would only delay the inevitable. There is no other way.

His voice again, heavy with hurt, but trusting still, "Father, if it is possible, may this cup be taken from Me. Yet not as I will, but as You will."

I nod toward the angel at My right hand and in an instant He is kneeling beside Jesus, strengthening Him. By now My Son's sweat is like drops of blood falling to the ground. His words tear at My heart, but there is nothing I can do.

"Abba, Father," He says, "everything is possible for You...."

If only that were true!

With a word, I call worlds into existence. At My command darkness is turned into light and order comes out of chaos. I make the barren womb fruitful and give the childless children. I speak from a bush that burns, but is not consumed. I turn rivers into blood and divide the sea so that My people may pass over on dry ground. By My Spirit the virgin conceives and the Son of God becomes the Son of Man, but I cannot grant Jesus' desperate plea.

Everything is possible for Me—everything, that is, except this!

Being absolutely just, I cannot allow a single sin to go unpunished; nor can I forgive a solitary sinner until My justice is fully satisfied, until every sin—past, present, and future—is punished.

At the same time, I am also merciful and I cannot turn My back on Adam's lost race. If I were to do so, I would betray that part of My eternal character. Because of Who I am, I am compelled to satisfy both My justice and My mercy.

Herein lies the dilemma: How can I be both just and merciful? How can I forgive Adam's sinful race without betraying the just demands of My holy name? Moreover, how can I judge their sins without denying My love and mercy?

The cross is the only answer, for in the cross both My mercy and My justice will be fully vindicated. Through His sacrificial death, Jesus will manifest My unconditional love, even as He suffers the full penalty for humanity's sins, thus satisfying the just demands of My righteous character.

He speaks again, no longer pleading, but submissive and obedient, "My Father, if it is not possible for this cup to be taken away unless I drink it, may Your will be done."

With trembling hands, He takes the cup, drinks deeply of its deadly dregs, and the final act begins. From eternity I watch as redemption's drama unfolds. It is a script prepared in eternity past. I know its scenes well, having created them Myself—yet the stark reality of this dreadful moment rips at My heart.

Now the executioner places a five-inch iron spike against the outstretched hand of My only begotten Son. As he raises his huge hammer, I find myself longing for another way, a plan that would save both My beloved Son and Me from this awful hour. But in eternity there is only silence, for there is no other way, and there is no other sacrifice for the sins of Adam's race.

Finally, the tortured silence is shattered by the sound of a solitary hammer striking a nail, and Jesus is crucified. His life blood spills out as a ransom for lost men and women. He suffers the full penalty for Adam's sin.

Watching My beloved Son writhe in the agonies of crucifixion's slow death, I am torn with conflicting emotions. A part of Me longs to tear the darkness away, to gently lift His trembling body from the cross. Oh that I might end His sufferings, that I might bathe His wounds with My tears.

Yet, another part of Me is nearly in awe, witnessing His sacrificial love. Never has there been anything like this, not in time or eternity.

As the sixth hour approaches, darkness descends. In an act reminiscent of the day of atonement, I place My hands upon His bloodied head and, in a voice only He can hear, I impute to Him all the sins of Adam's lost race. In the deepening darkness, My sinless Son becomes the greatest sinner in time or eternity.

During the three hours of light, He suffered at the hands of wicked men. In the three hours of darkness, He suffers at My holy hand. During the three hours of light, He suffered man's injustice. In the three hours of darkness, He suffers My divine justice. During the three hours of light, He suffered as the innocent for the guilty. In the three hours of darkness, He suffers not only as the condemned for sin, but as sin itself!

In order to reconcile the world to Myself, I must banish Jesus from My presence. He must suffer the full retribution for the sins of mankind. Therefore, with determined deliberateness, I turn My back on Him. I abandon Him. This is the ultimate punishment: separation from My holy presence.

Though He bore the brutality of the Roman whip without a whimper and suffered the cruelty of the cross without uttering a word, this separation is more than He can bear in silence. Alone in the darkness, He screams, "My God, My God, why have You forsaken Me?"

I will Myself not to hear, but it is no use. There is no escaping His haunting cry. On this day, We will each suffer in Our own way. He—judgment at My hand, and I—His haunting cry!

To see My Son suffer at the hands of sinful men was nearly more than I could bear, but it was nothing compared to this. Now I am the perpetrator of His pain, the source of His agony. I have smitten Him and afflicted His soul. I have crushed Him and laid upon Him the iniquity of all mankind. I have made His life an offering for sin. I have cut Him off from the land of the living, made Him pour out His soul unto death. I have forsaken Him, inflicting a pain like no other. At My hands He has suffered the torments of the damned!

Finally, it is over and in death He triumphs. Though I have not relented nor displayed even a hint of mercy toward Him, He still trusts Me. With His dying breath, He offers Me His soul.

And now I hear Him call My Name, "Father," He says, "into Your hands I commit My spirit."

It is finished!

Sin's debt is finally paid. My holy justice is fully satisfied. At last I am free to forgive every son and daughter of Adam! It makes no difference how far they may have fallen or the sinful deeds they may have done.

Only one thing remains and I now turn My attention to the temple in Jerusalem. Laying hold of the curtain, separating the holy place from the holy of holies where My presence abides, I tear it in two from top to bottom. Never again will anything other than unbelief separate Me from Adam's race. Now and forever I am as near as the smallest prayer whispered in Jesus' name.

Life Lessons

1. Maybe you have never experienced the love of a father such as I have shared in the stories of this section. Perhaps you have no father or your relationship with your father has been marred by actions that have created deep wounds.
2. God is real. He not only wants to heal those wounds, He wants to embrace you as a Father. He stands waiting. The choice is up to you.
3. Will you pray now?

Father, I now realize the sacrifice You made for me. How You were willing to watch as Your Son, Jesus Christ, died an excruciating death, all to pay the price for my sin. I believe in You. I accept the gift of eternal life that You offer to all who believe. I repent. Please show me who You really are. Amen.

A Note from the Author

I hope the stories in *Seasons of Love* have brought both joy and encouragement to your life. If so, I will have accomplished the first part of my mission. By purchasing this book, you are helping me accomplish the second part. The royalties from *Seasons of Love* will be used to fund ongoing ministry endeavors in Asia where my husband and I have worked for the past fifteen years.

If you prayed the prayer at the end of the book or have just enjoyed reading these stories, I would love to hear from you. Or if you would like information on how you can join us in ministry to the 10/40 window in Asia, please contact me:

Karen Hardin

P. O. Box 700515

Tulsa, OK 74170-0515

khardin@gorilla.net

About the Author

Karen Hardin is a freelance writer, seasoned missionary, and busy mom. Her work has appeared in *USA Today, Charisma, Fresh Outlook* magazine, *Make Your Day Count for Teachers,* and more. Her first book in this series, *Seasons of Life for Women,* was released in March 2004. She and her husband, Kevin, have ministered in Asia for the past fifteen years, living there for seven of them. In addition to home-schooling their three children, Karen manages her own publicity firm. For additional information on the Hardin's work in Asia, visit www.chcall.org.

About the Artist

Nancy Harkins has excelled in painting and drawing since she was a young child and is primarily self-taught. Her watercolors have received awards in national and regional exhibitions and are in private and corporate collections around the country. They have been chosen for publication by the American Iris Society, Voice of the Martyrs Ministries, and North Light Books. She has also had the honor of showing her work at Gilcrease Museum in Tulsa, Oklahoma. She resides in Tulsa with her husband and best friend, Ed.

If you have enjoyed this book,
we would love to hear from you!

Visit our Web site at:
www.whitestonebooks.com

Additional copies of this title
are available from your local bookstore.

Also available in the series:

Season of Life:
Reflections to Celebrate the Heart of a Woman

Seasons of Hope:
Experiencing the Miracle of God's Grace
(Coming soon!)

"... To him who overcomes
I will give some of the hidden manna to eat.
And I will give him a white stone,
and on the stone a new name written
which no one knows except him who receives it."
REVELATION 2:17 NKJV

WHITE STONE BOOKS
LAKELAND, FLORIDA

If you have enjoyed this book,
we would love to hear from you!

Additional copies of this title
are available from your local bookstore.

Also available in the series:

Season of Life:
Reflections to Celebrate the Heart of a Woman

Seasons of Hope:
Experiencing the Miracle of God's Grace
(Coming soon!)

"... To him who overcomes
I will give some of the hidden manna to eat.
And I will give him a white stone,
and on the stone a new name written
which no one knows except him who receives it."
REVELATION 2:17 NKJV

WS
WHITE STONE BOOKS
LAKELAND, FLORIDA